PRAISE FOR:

SOARING ABOVE THE ASHES ON THE WINGS OF FORGIVENESS

Offering the *restoration of hope* has been the premise of my forty-year career working with high-risk, drug and gang impacted youth, couples and families. Kitty Chappell's book on forgiveness has become an invaluable resource providing concrete evidence that healing is possible. It should be in the 'tool box' of anyone with a heart for helping families both *in* and *outside* the church!

—Dan Villarreal,
Strengthening Families Program Director,
Former Probation and Parole Officer

Kitty Chappell's skill at writing, her honesty in telling her story, and her transparency in sharing her pain, combine to make *Soaring Above the Ashes on the Wings of Forgiveness*, a compelling read. As each page reveals her life you will say, "It can't be true." By the time you finish, you too may be able to forgive!

– Doug Ross,
President Emeritus Evangelical
Christian Publishers Association

Soaring Above the Ashes on the Wings of Forgiveness is a must-read! After its translation into Polish, Kitty shared her amazing story throughout thirteen of our cities where she was a living example that each of us, with God's help, can forgive anyone. This inspiring book challenges us to be overcomers, not mere survivors—and it shows us how.

—Jagoda Markiewicz,
Women's Forum Director
Warsaw, Poland

Kitty is not only a survivor, she is a hero. Her horrifying childhood makes her ability to forgive even more powerful. I learned so much from her wisdom and her heart. No one has to be a victim. Kitty teaches us how to soar.

—Karen Covell,
Television producer,
coauthor of *The Day I Met God*

Kitty Chappell writes her powerful true life story in such a way that it is hard to put her book down, hard to not be involved, and almost impossible to not be transformed!

—Moises Menezes,
Filmmaker
Warsaw, Poland

In a world filled with conflict and grievances at every level, Kitty Chappell's compelling personal story book, *Soaring Above the Ashes on the Wings of Forgiveness,* reminds us that even when life isn't fair, things change when we choose to forgive. Most importantly, we change.

—Mark Gilroy,
Author of *Cuts Like a Knife*

Kitty's story shook me to my core, and her path to forgiveness has provided a beacon of light that helps illuminate my way each and every day. If you seek an author who can touch your life in a powerful, positive and personal way, look no farther than Kitty Chappell and her book, *Soaring Above the Ashes on the Wings of Forgiveness.*

—Tim Winter
President, Parents Television Council

Bitterness and resentment can gnaw away at our souls if we don't find forgiveness in our hearts. Kitty Chappell not only survived but overcame her painful circumstances, and this is her story.

—Susan Titus Osborn,
Author of *The Complete Guide to Christian Writing and Speaking*

Nothing compares with divine forgiveness and the invitation to live it as revealed in Kitty Chappell's life story *Soaring Above the Ashes on the Wings of Forgiveness.* It was a blessing for me to translate this powerful book into the Nepali language—then observe how it helps our people to victoriously overcome trauma and injustice.

—D.P. Khanal (Divya),
(former Braham Hindu)
Deacon, The Lord's Assembly,
Kathmandu, Nepal

In *Soaring Above the Ashes on the Wings of Forgiveness,* Kitty Chappell presents a stirring testimony of God's grace and reveals practical application of obedience to His command that we forgive others as He forgives us. The reward in this true drama is the author's ultimate personal freedom and restoration. This book provides hope and help for all who struggle with the need to forgive.

—Prema Caruna, M.D.,
Doctor of Medicine and Psychiatry

May you always soar!

Kitty Chappell

SOARING ABOVE THE ASHES ON THE WINGS OF FORGIVENESS

SOARING ABOVE THE ASHES ON THE WINGS OF FORGIVENESS

KITTY CHAPPELL

TATE PUBLISHING
AND **ENTERPRISES,** LLC

Published by Tate Publishing & Enterprises, LLC
127 E. Trade Center Terrace | Mustang, Oklahoma 73064 USA
1.888.361.9473 | www.tatepublishing.com

Tate Publishing is committed to excellence in the publishing industry. The company reflects the philosophy established by the founders, based on Psalm 68:11, *"The Lord gave the word and great was the company of those who published it."*

Book design copyright © 2013 by Tate Publishing, LLC. All rights reserved.
Cover design by Rodrigo Adolfo
Interior design by Joana Quilantang

Published in the United States of America

ISBN: 978-1-62563-053-7
1. Biography & Autobiography / Personal Memoirs
2. Family & Relationships / Abuse / General
13.02.06

This book was formerly published under the title of *Sins of a Father—Forgiving the Unforgivable.*

Some names have been changed to protect the privacy of certain individuals.

To my brother, Chuck, and my sister, Chris, who can say with me: "Don't let evil conquer you, but conquer evil by doing good"

(Romans 12:21).

ACKNOWLEDGMENTS

Each of us is an artist. Our thoughts, words, and actions are the brushstrokes used to help paint not only our self-image, but those of others. I thank God for the trustworthy artists in my life, friends and relatives who through the years have applied warm-colored words of encouragement and praise, layer by layer, upon the canvas of my mind—a craft executed in love.

I am grateful for the godly ministers, Sunday school teachers, and fellow Christians in my life who "walked their talk," leaving golden footprints across my mind.

I thank God for one exceptional artist—my ever-praying maternal grandmother. Her glowing words of affirmation in my dark environment made me feel I had value, regardless of my performance. In the early years of my mind, she faithfully placed diamond-studded Scriptures into its every nook and cranny then covered them with prayer. They lay there ready to shine with the brilliance of understanding when the light of Christ flooded my soul at the age of fourteen.

I thank God also for the negative strokes, the black-and-blue bruises on my soul, the razor-sharp edges of actions and remarks that cut to the core of my mind's canvas, letting the bright red from my wounds bleed through. Without the penetration of ugly experiences, there would have been no crimson to seep through and blend with the darker colors to form God's perfect color of purple compassion.

I am grateful that nothing is wasted in God's economy. He has helped me to use the brushstrokes of good and evil alike, friends and foes, to help paint my character into a self-image worth viewing—that of a joyful overcomer. Special heartwarming thanks go to the dear ones listed below:

Joan Englander—the reporter who first wrote my story in her Ojai, California, newspaper column in 1982. Meeting her was divinely orchestrated—a meeting that set into motion a chain of events that is still at work.

Gerry King—my sweet friend and area representative for Stonecroft Ministries. After she read Joan's article, she encouraged me to become a speaker to Christian Women's Clubs and After-Five Christian Women's Business and Professional Groups. As a result, for more than twenty-five years I have shared the good news with thousands of women throughout the U.S. that they too can become overcomers.

Betty Arthurs—a fellow writer, as well as other dear friends in the Tuesday's Children Professional Christian Writer's Group. With fear and trepidation, I handed Betty my first chapter (the only one I had written) for her "absolutely honest" opinion. Had there been even the slightest sign of negative body language on her part, another layer of doubt would have been added to my already-fearful mind that this book would be boring—and I probably would have shelved the idea. But her spontaneous response of, "This is awesome!" splashed bright strokes of hope in my heart, so I continued.

Etta Mae Pickens—my fiercest prayer warrior. At just the right moments, when I felt like giving up, the phone would ring and I'd hear her sweet voice reminding me that she was praying for me every day.

Shawna Bedal—I appreciate so much Shawna's invaluable help with Scripture research.

New Hope Publishers—who published the original edition of this book under the title of *Sins of a Father, Forgiving the Unforgivable.* I am forever indebted to them.

Vocatio Publishers, Warsaw Poland—I will be eternally grateful to president and CEO Piotr Waclawik for his faith in *Sins of a Father, Forgiving the Unforgivable.* Vocatio was responsible for retitling it as *I Can Forgive if I Want to*, and its publication in six languages to date.

Tate Publishers—The words "thank you" are definitely inadequate to express my deep gratitude for their enthusiastic acceptance of this updated and revised edition of my life story. Tate's strong belief in its message led to the publishing of *Soaring above the Ashes on the Wings of Forgiveness*—thereby giving it new wings to soar again!

Hannah Tranberg—without her skill and insight, this book would be less than it is.

Peggy Levesque—loving friend and fellow writer helped immensely by reformatting this book when I was crunched for time and energy.

Carole Barnes—dear friend and founder of CBA Speakers Bureau, graciously took time from her busy schedule to assist in photo preparation for the photo section in this book.

Pat Harris—my dearest friend of many years (I can't tell you how many because she swears she's not that old) has been my strongest supporter.

Jerry Chappell—my late husband for forty-seven wonderful years was my greatest admirer and supporter. I am thankful he didn't leave me during the writing of the first edition of this book—and grateful for his patience, which was sorely tried at times. Once he ventured into my office, despite its warning sign that read "Disaster Area," and timidly asked, "Honey, are you ever going to the store again?"

TABLE OF CONTENTS

INTRODUCTION

Who hasn't been hurt by someone, somewhere, at sometime? Who hasn't felt the sting of injustice, the emptiness of rejection, and the soul-gnawing presence of hate and resentment?

While not every individual has experienced abuse in the strongest sense of the word, each of us has felt abused and mistreated and succumbed to self-pity at one time or another. But beware! Self-pity is the stuff that the victim mentality is made of. If allowed to ferment, age, and grow, self-pity can create a prison in which its victims suffer damage far greater than that inflicted by any perpetrator—a prison that fosters bitterness, not betterment.

This book is about surviving and overcoming. There are millions of survivors but few overcomers. What is the difference between a survivor and an overcomer? Survivors live through their heartbreaking circumstances but never get beyond their pain. They live but they are not alive. They remain trapped in their victimhood, blaming others for their problems. Some robe themselves in self-pity and drag their hurts behind them like dirty, tattered security blankets—defying anyone to step on them. Others blast fiery charges of hate into innocent bystanders—either with words or with bullets. And at the end of the day, they curse their misery as they stare blankly through the bars of a prison fashioned by their own flawed thinking. They do not see the key hanging by their window—the key to freedom.

Overcomers have also survived heartbreak and pain, but they have discovered the key within their grasp and use it wisely. They unlock the doors of their past and use its stumbling blocks as stepping stones to freedom. They exchange their tattered robes of self-pity for clean and practical garments of accountability. They walk in strength and grace. They rejoice in the fresh air of their freedom and the sunrise of their joy, for they know that neither heartache nor tragedy will ever again hold them prisoner.

While this book contains heartache, horror, and disappointment, it is about hope and overcoming. It was not written by a group of detached observers of pain or by a professional panel who discussed and debated theories as to how those who have been deeply wounded should deal with their pain. Nor is it a "somebody done me wrong but I survived anyway" book. It is a story of God's power and grace.

This book was written by an individual who was born into an environment of violence, experienced the pain of abuse and the ravages of rage and resentment yet emerged not as a mere survivor but as a victorious overcomer. As a speaker to women's groups for over twenty-five years, I became increasingly aware that most of us need help in letting go of our hurts. We need assistance in developing accountability to God and man if ever we hope to overcome our pain and become all God intends us to be—and deep in our hearts, we long to be.

PART I

SINS OF A FATHER

Heavy with grief and guilt, I wept silently, thoughts churning as I stared at the two caskets flanking each other on their stands.

Should I have shot him long ago as I had planned? If I had, none of this would have happened.

One, laden with flowers, proclaimed from its satin banner, "Our beloved mother and sister," was my stepmother. The second bore no banner. Just a single red rose, a solitary reminder that the remains inside were my father.

Had I failed again? Could I have prevented this?

Dad had always been violent. My earliest memories were cringing in a corner, holding my hands over my ears as my father repeatedly beat my mother. But nothing I did could shut out her screams.

When I was a three and a half years old, I fell madly in love with an adorable baby named Charles. He had the brightest blue eyes I'd ever seen—my new baby brother. With his perfectly shaped head covered with blond fuzz, he looked just like a doll, my doll. Even though I was a mere toddler, I recall feeling strangely protective of this new addition to our family—a feeling that would last the rest of my life.

When I was seven and a half years old, our sister, Christine, was born and I fell in love a second time. Tiny, blue-eyed, and also blond, her delicate features reminded me of the porcelain China doll mother treasured so much. Again, I felt this strong bond of protection. This fierce love lured me into the mother role, not only for my siblings, but, later on, also for our young mother, a mere fifteen years older than I.

Children are never too young to be affected by their environment. As a toddler, Charles often crawled out of his cot during the night and sleepwalked toward the front door. In wide-eyed terror, whimpering like a frightened puppy, he clawed at it with quick doglike strokes—futile attempts of a tiny boy subconsciously trying to escape his environment.

It was my responsibility to get Charles back onto his cot quickly, since Mom feared any movement on her part might awaken Dad. But sometimes I slept too soundly and failed to reach him in time. Angered by his disruption of sleep, Dad would bound out of bed, grab Chuck's frail body, and beat him with a leather belt, mumbling, "I'll teach the little...to wake me up!"

"Clyde, please don't, he's just a baby," Mother cried out, grabbing at Dad's arms.

"Shut up, Esther! Stay out of this!"

"But he doesn't realize what he's doing—he's sleepwalking," Mom begged.

"Then this will wake him up!" Dad snarled.

Mom's attempts to intervene always ended the same. She was knocked to the floor, where she lay frozen in fear. She knew any further attempts to help Charles would result in Dad beating him even harder.

I flinched as I heard the thick leather strap slapping against Charles's frail, bony frame. His screams pierced the stillness of the night and stabbed my heart with deeper guilt. I lay there motionless, afraid to breathe. Once I heard the rhythmic sound of Dad's deep breathing, I crept to Charles's cot and stroked his wet face. My tears blended with his as I whispered, "I'm so sorry I didn't wake up in time." Who could know that this sleeping toddler boy would one day, in his teens, lay in wait planning to shoot his father?

FINDING BEAUTY
IN CHAOS

After accepting a job as foreman of a large farm, Dad moved us from Fulton, Arkansas, the birthplace of Charles and Chris, to the lush and fertile river bottoms bordering the Red River. Our rented house was built high upon stilts as an attempt to prevent damage from flooding when the swollen and angry Red River overflowed its banks. That preventative measure didn't always work. Fortunately, however, our house was flooded only twice while we lived there. Although being evacuated from our home was frightening, it was at the same time rather exciting to me. Not so to Mom and Dad, who had to shovel out the red sand and silt from our wooden floors once the waters receded.

We were happy when Dad was away overseeing the farm, riding his horse, Star. The balmy summers there (and later in East Texas) afforded pleasant diversions from our violent home life—beautiful experiences that provided positive memory tools we used to momentarily block out our pain and replace bitter memories of our youth after we were grown. Our fun-loving mother played a central role in creating these positive memories. And I'm sure she needed these experiences as much as we did.

Mom instilled in us a love and respect for nature that remains with us today. She taught us to identify wild birds and recognize their calls, even mimic their sounds. We learned the names of wildflowers and delighted in surprising her with fresh bouquets, especially the pale blue wood violets that peeked out from under dead tree leaves in the spring. Wild honeysuckle was my favorite. But we quickly learned to avoid the bright yellow bitterweeds plants—in fact, we detested them! We knew firsthand the bitterness of a cow's milk if she had grazed in an area containing even a few of those toxic plants, which could be fatal if she ate too many.

Mom showed us the fun of kneeling in the red sand and twirling a thin straw in delicate circles in the center of the nest where the doodle bugs lived. We'd excitedly chant the refrain, "Doodle bug, doodle bug, your house is on fire!" The doodle bug poked its head and upper half of body out of its sandpit expectantly. On close examination, it resembled a dinosaur with its fusiform body and tiny pincers. Then we'd excitedly shout, "Doodlebug, doodlebug, run back home. Your house is on fire, and your kids'r all alone!"

As it dove back into the sand we doubled over with laughter, shaking with deep and exaggerated belly laughs, pretending it was funnier than it actually was—our attempts to glean as much joy as possible from these pleasant experiences. Years later, we learned that what we called doodle bugs were really antlions—tiny anteaters belonging to a family of insects called Myrmeleontidae. (They were actually the larvae.) We were disappointed to realize our warning about her house being on fire was not the motivation for her quick appearance, but her anticipation of catching a nice juicy ant. And I'm sure her disappointment was keener than ours.

The summer before I started fourth grade, Dad accepted a position twenty-three miles west of Fulton at the Red River Military Arsenal in Texarkana, Texas. He made a down payment on a house located in the suburbs on an old but beautiful tree-lined street at 1618 Oak Street. We were so excited! No more renting. This was our very own home—our first one—and nobody could kick us out! We were especially delighted over the fruit trees in the backyard where we later enjoyed their generous yield of mulberries, figs, pomegranates, purple plums, and, in particular, a Concord grape arbor where we could sit on a wooden bench beneath it and pluck sweet juicy grapes. (I often took pomegranates to school, where I sold them to classmates for extra money—a quarter for medium size and fifty cents for the large ones.)

Each year Mom grew a beautiful garden that provided long, slender carrots so crunchy and sweet we would often pull them up from the loamy soil, rinse them off with the garden hose and eat them right there. Cucumbers, squash, large sweet Bermuda onions, pole beans, okra, green onions, radishes, several types of lettuce, garlic, and juicy tomatoes enticed our taste buds into enjoying vegetables. We loved Mom's wilted salads topped with crumbled bacon pieces and covered with sizzling bacon drippings. The vine-ripened tomatoes were my favorite, so full of flavor that nothing else was needed in a sandwich—just mayonnaise and big juicy slices of tomatoes, salted and peppered a little. I would sit on the back porch stoop and munch away as the juice ran down my wrists.

Texarkana is a twin city, straddling the Arkansas and Texas border where the state line runs smack dab through the middle of town. Later, as a teenager, I enjoyed shopping downtown with my teenage friends. Before buying a dress we liked on the Texas side, we'd walk across the street into Arkansas to see if we could find the same dress there. If we did, we would purchase it on that side of the street because Arkansas had no sales tax at that time. I loved it when we'd go to the post office/court house because there were always friendly tourist couples who asked us to take their pictures side by side but each in a different state.

Charles and I quickly discovered the Swampoodle Creek several blocks from our house located just on the outskirts of town. Mom taught us to tie a string to the end of a long stick, secure pieces of pork rind to the end, and drop it into the murky waters and catch large crawdads. Sometimes we'd bring up several at a time when competing claws got entangled. This fun pastime provided great entertainment for us two kids, while Mom and little Chris wandered around checking out wildflowers, pretty rocks, and looking for bird's nests. Mom always cooked the crawdads after we proudly carried them home. (Years later, as an adult, I would order crayfish at restaurants serving authentic Cajun cuisine, preferring its rich flavor to that of shrimp.)

We loved visiting our maternal grandmother and stepgrandfather, who lived in the edge of the Ozarks near Hatfield, Arkansas, where the nearby streams were crystal clear. After our maternal Grandpa George Wesley Watson passed away, our granny, whose full name was Mary Elizabeth Hunt-Watson, married William McAllister and moved to this lovely farm. Though we missed Grandpa Watson, our new grandpa, known as "Willie" to everyone, quickly endeared himself to us as he welcomed us hurting children into his big heart. How we looked forward to our visits with them at the farm—heaven away from hell!

There were no modern amenities at the farm—no electricity, gas, or running water. Two springs at the bottom of the hill beside their house was their only source of water. The water in one spring was used only for washing clothes and bathing as it was not potable. All water had to be carried in buckets from the springs up to the house. Any water needing to be heated was done so in a large tea kettle on the wood cook stove. For our baths, Granny gradually added steaming hot water to cold water in the stainless steel wash tub outside and we took turns bathing—each of us wanting to be first. Serious bathing only occurred once a week on Saturday nights so we'd be clean for church the next morning. (We swam often in the nearby crystal clear Mt. Fork River, so we never got too dirty.)

During summer visits, we children helped Granny shell fresh butter beans and black eyed peas from their garden. A wild strawberry patch yielding the sweetest strawberries I had ever tasted grew just beyond the garden fence. Though these were much smaller than the commercially raised strawberries, their flavor made up for their lack in size.

When wild blackberries were in season, we'd take our buckets and brave the briars, ticks, and chiggers beyond the creek to pick as many as we could knowing we'd be rewarded with one of

Granny's famous blackberry cobblers. One of my fondest memories was when Jack Bramer, one of our cousins several years older than I, joined us in our berry-picking ventures during his visits to the farm. Jack often would burst into song a few yards away, substituting his own lyrics to *The Cowboy's Lament* ballad about not wanting to be buried on the lone prairie. "Oh, bury me not in the blackberry patch, where the chiggers bite and the people scratch."

At the farm, I loved gathering the eggs each day and filling a basket. Some of the chickens preferred to not use the hen house nests and had their own unique locations to lay their eggs. One hen made her nest in the weeds by a fence post, another in an old rusty metal barrel turned on its side, and several others had spots in the barn hay loft. Most of them, however, preferred the security of the hen house in the corner of the back yard behind the house. I loved hunting for the eggs, however. It was like enjoying an Easter egg hunt all year round.

It was mostly my chore during our visits there to keep the water buckets filled. The stainless steel buckets hang on hooks attached to slender wire cables suspended from the kitchen ceiling over a stand with a metal pan or basin for washing our hands. One of the buckets always contained a long-handled dipper for drinking. When water got low in the first bucket, we moved the dipper to the next bucket until a run to the spring was made. Nobody seemed to worry about germs back then for everyone drank from the same dipper and tossed any remaining water into the pan below for hand washing. The stand stood in the kitchen next to the back door. During hot summer days, both doors, front and back, were propped open so the house could be cooled by the mountain breezes. Granny propped the back door open with one of her heavy clothes irons that she had to heat on the cook stove before doing her ironing. The front door was propped open with a more formal door stop, a huge piece of beautiful quartz rock found on the farm in earlier years. Roaming the woods on this farm was literally a treasure hunt for us kids with its abundance of rock quartz crystals and authentic arrowheads.

Making my water runs to the spring was no easy task, but I never minded—mostly because it put me in contact with two creeks. I think Grandpa's love for me was sorely tried at times due to my crawdad-catching addiction. When one of the water buckets emptied, I unhooked it, carried it out the back door, around the side of the house, through the side yard gate, down the hill, and crossed my favorite creek on a plank used as a bridge. Quite often, I stopped, caught, and played with the crawdads for a while. Then I continued on down, passing the non-potable spring, and on a few yards beyond to the drinking spring, where I hunkered down to fill my bucket.

Grandpa taught me to never put my hands in this small pool of crystal clear water gurgling up from the rocks, because that was our drinking water. Instead, I submerged a portion of the bucket and let it slowly fill without my hands touching the water. My biggest challenge, however, was ignoring the largest and prettiest crawdads I'd ever seen in my life. Their distinct and unique markings, seen nowhere else other than this spring, mesmerized me as they rested lazily on the side rocks just beneath the water surface. I was sure they were gloating as they looked up at me and never even tried to scamper away. They seemed to know I wasn't supposed to touch them. What a temptation! Sometimes, just as my hand hovered over the water, ready to snatch one of them, Grandpa Willie would step out on the front porch and yell, "Cathleen!" (I didn't get the nickname of "Kitty" until I was around thirteen.) "You're not trying to catch those crawdads, are you?"

To which I always lied by replying, "No sir," as I quickly grabbed the bucket and started my uphill return.

Fortunately for those who drank the water I drew from the spring, I spent most of my time crawfishing in the larger creek. While hiding under rocks, the crawdad's antennas could easily be seen in the clear running waters. I spent long hours catching these speedy creatures. After my first batch was rejected by Granny because they were too small to cook, I always returned them to their lovely cool waters. (I believe this sport was the primary reason I developed the quick reflexes that earned me the unofficial title among my friends as ping pong champion clear into adulthood.)

Though my reflexes were quick, they couldn't compare with Granny's! Sometimes, when Chuck and Chris were off someplace playing, Granny and I rested on the front porch of the old farmhouse built by Grandpa McAllister in his youth for his first wife, who died, and watched the tree squirrels play in the tall oak trees. Granny kept a slingshot on a peg on the front wall of the house. Many times she'd pick up a rock, put it in the slingshot, knock a squirrel out of the tree, and we'd have squirrel and dumplings for supper. One day as we sat on the front porch, Granny asked, "Cathleen, would you like to have squirrel and dumplings for supper tonight?"

"Yes!"

So she walked over to get the slingshot, but it wasn't on its peg. Undaunted, Granny picked up a hefty rock, drew back her arm, took aim, and like a professional baseball player, let it fly. A big fat squirrel never knew what hit him. It landed with a thud on the ground below—and I had my favorite meal for supper.

I took Granny's rock-throwing skills for granted as a child, but when I became a grandmother many years later, her prowess thoroughly impressed me! As my only grandchild and I sat watching the squirrels play in the tall oak tree near the outside deck of our Oakhurst, California home one afternoon, I was reminded of Granny McAllister's skill with the slingshot and rocks. I related these stories to five-year-old Bailey, the only child of our son David. Bailey listened wide-eyed, eyes darting between the fat gray tree squirrels in the tree and me. Finally she asked, "Can you do that, Grandma Kitty?"

I replied, "Honey, if your supper depended upon me knocking a squirrel out of that tree, I'm afraid you would starve!"

On warm summer afternoons, we caught lazy June bugs, tied strings to their legs, and flew them around like kites. I cherished those balmy nights at the farm where Chuck, Chris, and I chased lightning bugs that lit up the blue Mason jars we carried. I loved playing hopscotch with my favorite McAllister cousin, Maralyn Posey, until it got too dark for us to see our markers of broken pieces of glass.

Once we had sponge bathed and were in our pajamas, Granny read Bible stories from her tattered old Bible by the light of the kerosene lamp. After proclaiming God's unfailing love, she always knelt with us as we each said our prayers, her arms stretched around us as far as they could reach. Never did we feel so safe and secure as we drifted off to sleep while there at Granny and Grandpa's.

It was those lovely McAllister farm memories that Chuck, Chris, and I tried to focus on as we lay in our beds during the dark nights of trembling as we listened to the helpless cries of our mother. In each of our minds, we silently pled the same futile plea, "Please, Daddy, stop beating Mommy!" And for who-knows-what this time? Burning his dinner? Putting too much starch on his shirts? "Disobeying" him in some way? Or simply because he found a fresh cigarette butt left on the ground by the side of our house by a meter reader.

THE UNHAPPY BIRTHDAY WISH

"Happy birthday, Kitty. You are now officially a teenager!" Mother announced with a smile, eyes glowing with pride. Make a wish and blow out your candles, sweetheart."

I stared at the double-layered chocolate cake covered with fluffy white frosting. "Happy Birthday, Kitty" greeted me in cherry pink script letters with tiny matching flowers dotting every *I* from the center of the cake. Pink flowers with tiny green leaves danced around its sides, while thirteen pale green candles, placed evenly around the cake top, guarded the flowers below.

"It is so beautiful, Mom! Thank you."

Birthdays were special to our mother. She had never missed baking us our favorite cake, and as far back as I could remember, she had encouraged us to invite our friends over for a party. But not this time.

As special as turning thirteen was for me, I had declined a party at the last minute because I didn't want Mom to be embarrassed. Her right eye was swollen and black, with prominent bruises on her right jaw. I knew she would lie to cover up for Dad, and I couldn't stomach that. Not again.

I closed my eyes and made my wish. *I wish my father were dead!*

Despite Mother's gaiety, the scene was somber. I glanced at Charles, whom we now called Chuck, hunched over the table, head bowed, resting on his knuckles, elbows rigid. I couldn't tell if his eyes were closed or if he was just staring at the patterns on the oilcloth. To my left sat six-year-old Chris, golden hair shining (she had given it extra brushes for this special occasion). Her eyes danced as she eyed the cake, eagerly waiting for me to cut the first slice, knowing she would get the next piece. Like a graceful butterfly, she waved her delicate arms, fanning the smoking candles before Mother and I gathered them onto a saucer.

Dad's place was empty. He had stormed from the table earlier, following his usual threats of punishment. He took advantage of meal times, when we were all together, to reprimand us of any misdeeds, perceived or real. Who could eat after receiving a pronouncement of the punishment that would be forthcoming once the meal was over? Birthdays were no exception.

"Hmmm, hmmm, it is so good! This is your best cake ever, Mom!" I exulted, glancing toward Chuck. I smacked loudly as I licked frosting from my fingers and placed the first moist slice onto my plate. I watched for Chuck's reaction, for I knew chocolate was also his favorite. Slowly he lifted his head and fixed his gaze on the edible vision beckoning from the center of the table. By the time I had placed an extra thick slice on his plate, the sparkle had returned to his sad blue eyes.

I was confused by Dad's cruelty and his inconsistency in showing it. While he appeared to love some of our pets, he would, without apparent provocation, kill others.

Late one Saturday afternoon I arrived home from babysitting all day for a neighbor down the street. The delicious aroma of frying chicken bombarded my hungry senses as I opened the door.

"Yum, that smells so good!" I called out to Mom as I walked into the kitchen. She didn't turn and greet me with her usual smile, nor did she answer. She just stood there at the stove, her back to me, rigid.

"Mom?" I said louder. "What's the matter?

Finally she turned a tear-streaked face to me. Unsmiling and blinking hard, she said, "Your little sister needs you."

"Why? What's wrong?"

Mom chewed her bottom lip, as if to keep from crying, and nodded toward Chris's room.

For a moment, I stood outside her door, listening to the soft sobs on the other side.

"Honey, it's me," I said, pushing the door open gently. Chris sat on the floor with her head in her arms on the side of her bed. She wore her favorite ruffled pinafore, the one that was so tedious to iron. She always tried, however, to not dirty it. When she jumped up, I was surprised to see long streaks of dark red stains splashed across its front.

Is that blood? My heart pounded. "What happened, honey, are you hurt?"

Suddenly Chris threw her arms around me, hugging me hard. Her body shook as she sobbed into my hair, "My Henrietta is dead!"

Oh, no. Not her favorite little pet!

A friend of the family had given each of us a dyed Easter chick the previous spring. They were the cutest, cuddliest creatures we had ever seen. Pink, blue, and orange fluff balls of joy that brightened our days. Chris immediately named her chick Henrietta, and they became inseparable. A month later, Chris proudly demonstrated how she had trained Henrietta to come on demand.

Each day, after arriving home from school, Chris rushed to the back door, threw it open, and called out, "Henrietta! Come, girl." Henrietta always came quickly and rubbed her feathered face against Chris's ankles, weaving excitedly in and out between them, until Chris scooped her up in her arms and they rubbed their faces together.

Only the soul of a child can understand the deep love bond between a pet and the heart that cherishes it, I had written in my diary that day. *All creatures respond to love, and every child needs the opportunity to express love.*

I thought of how Chris had poured all the pent-up love she carried for Father, who would never return it, upon a small creature who always returned it in full.

"My Henrietta," she often murmured in joy, stroking the satiny red feathers of her beloved pet, holding her close to her face. Henrietta, with closed eyes, obviously enjoyed those moments, for she never struggled to escape. It was with reluctance that she let Chris place her in the coop with the other two pet chickens at sundown, where she would be safe for the night.

"What happened?" I asked, pushing Chris away enough so I could see her face.

I was unprepared for her response. Chris's eyes narrowed. Through clenched teeth and trembling lips, she hissed, "Daddy killed her!"

Chris started shaking as the pent-up pain spilled from her overloaded heart. "He killed all of them! Our pets...yours,

Chuck's, and my Henrietta! And he made me watch! He wouldn't let me leave."

Oh, no! How could he!

Tears trickled onto Chris's hair as I held her close, both of us trembling. "I'm so sorry, honey," I cried, holding her tightly. But she needed to talk. She had to verbalize her story of horror.

"I went outside to let Henrietta out so I could play with her, but Daddy was already there, standing by the coop. He said he was waiting for me—told me to stay where I was, that he wanted me to watch something. Then he grabbed Blossom, your pet chicken, yanked her out of the cage, and closed the door. He held her up high and began wringing her neck. I started crying. I turned to run back inside, but he yelled, 'You stay right where you are, young lady! Don't you move!' Blossom was flopping around on the ground, dying, when he reached in and grabbed Chuck's chicken. When he did the same thing to Bessie, I knew he was saving my Henrietta for last."

Chris broke into loud sobs as she relived her tragic experience. I held her tightly, but there was no stopping her avalanche of pain. Its momentum pushed her headlong into the path of her story.

"I started screaming, 'Daddy, please don't hurt Henrietta!' But he wouldn't stop. I knew Henrietta was scared—she'd just watched her sisters die! And she was flapping her wings, trying to get out of the cage. I didn't want to watch Henrietta die too, but when I turned Daddy yelled again, 'You move one step, and I'll beat you within an inch of your life!' He reached into the back of the cage and grabbed Henrietta by the head. One of her wings got caught on the side of the opening, and she squawked. I knew it hurt her, but Daddy just yanked harder until she was out. He jerked her up and down by the head, swinging her around and around, moving closer and closer to me so I had to watch. Then he threw her to the ground so hard that her little neck broke completely off. Blood spurted everywhere, even on my dress."

My heart ached, and my throat burned from trying not to cry. *Poor little Chris—and she is so frightened at the sight of blood!*

"I started screaming louder but Daddy wouldn't let me move. 'Shut up!' he yelled, 'And don't close your eyes. It's not good for you kids to get so attached to things. So you watch!' Then he just stood there, smiling, while Henrietta's body kept flopping all around. I saw her little head lying in the grass, eyes still open, as if she had to watch too. I jumped when her body brushed against my legs, and Daddy laughed. I kept jumping around, stomping the ground hard, and trying to get the blood off me. I wanted to die. And Daddy just laughed harder!"

Emotionally spent, Chris buried her face in my chest and sobbed quietly, her breath catching every so often. I sat on the side of the bed with Chris huddled in my lap, my arms wrapped around her. I rocked her side to side in stoic silence. What could I say that could ease her intense pain?

Suddenly, fresh horror intruded my numb heart as a new realization pummeled my mind. *Oh, no! No wonder Mom was upset! Mom, who nurtures every injured wild bird we drag in back to health and who loves anything with feathers on it, was forced by Dad to prepare and cook our pets! How terrible for her! And how will we ever get through the evening meal!*

A deathly pall hung over the supper table as we picked at our food. Only our father seemed to relish every bite, smacking loudly, slurping the grease from his fingers. Not even with threat of a beating would Chris touch the piece of chicken set before her. To distract Dad's wary eyes from her every movement, the rest of us ripped our meat apart, spreading it around on our plates with exaggerated motion, but not eating it. We nibbled at our vegetables while Chris moved her fork slowly through her mashed potatoes and separated her green beans.

Fortunately, Dad didn't notice that Chris wasn't eating.

When Chris started to throw up, she was finally allowed to leave the table. As she ran for the bathroom, Dad called loudly after her, "This is the best chicken dinner I ever ate!" Then rubbing his belly, he laughed.

I had experienced hate for my father prior to this, but nothing prepared me for the repulsion that seared my soul. While Dad pushed a pile of bones onto a side plate, I placed my hands quickly out of sight under the table where they involuntarily doubled into tight fists. Inwardly, I screamed in rage, *I hate you! Someday, I'm going to kill you!*

By the time I was fourteen, hate for my father was full blown. I felt trapped and helpless. I often awoke exhausted from recurring nightmares in which my hands were tied behind my back and I was ordered to do something. "But I can't. My hands are tied!" I cried out. Nameless voices kept demanding that I do simple tasks that I couldn't do because of my tethered hands. Many times I was awakened by my groans and heard my voice pleading, "But I can't, I can't." I dreaded going to sleep.

I finally realized that no matter how much I wanted to, I could not protect my family. Though I daydreamed of ways for us to escape, I knew it was impossible. Dad had warned us too many times to not "go mouthing off to anyone about things that are none of their business, or I'll put you all out of your misery." Dad felt secure in our Texas town where he was well liked. "And you can be sure that no jury would ever convict me," he bragged. "I'd just plead temporary insanity."

No one, including my closest friends, suspected the truth. They had no idea of the terror we experienced behind the closed doors of our rose-covered house and well-trimmed lawn. To them, I was just an ordinary happy-go-lucky teenager with no worries other than what clothes to wear or which boy to dream of dating.

So picture-perfect did our lives appear that some of my friends expressed open envy.

"You are so lucky, Kitty!" a classmate remarked one day. Your mother is young and pretty, fun to be around, and your father is the most handsome man I know—such gorgeous blue eyes and wavy brown hair. I am so envious! I wish I were you."

My mouth dropped open in shock. "Don't ever wish you were someone else," I said brusquely. Taking her by the shoulders and shaking her, I added, "Be thankful you are who you are and for the life you live."

She looked at me strangely as tears filled my eyes before I turned and quickly walked away.

Though I succeeded in hiding my fear and hate behind my smile and quick sense of humor, I knew I couldn't live this way much longer. Something had to be done. But what? What choices did I have?

I was born and grew up during a time when our nation still reeled from the effects of the Great Depression. There were no shelters for battered women and children and no agencies to provide financial aid or free legal counsel. The prevailing attitude of abused women at that time was the one expressed by my mother when she often said, "Decent people don't air their dirty laundry in front of others." Besides, Dad had warned us not to tell anyone, and even if we did, what could an outsider do? We were on our own.

I was frustrated. I sought reasons for our father's abusive behavior, but no matter how hard I looked, I couldn't find any. Not one.

Our mother was sweet and gentle, loved to laugh, an excellent cook, good housekeeper, wonderful mother, beautiful with a school-girlish figure, and everyone loved her. She wasn't mean and never nagged our father—at least, not until she'd suffered many long years of abuse. By the time I entered my teens, Mom was determined to have her say even if it meant she'd be beaten for it. It was the only weapon she had that could inflict any kind of discomfort on our father, albeit a poor one—one that prompted more beatings and caused us more misery. Many times in the latter years of their marriage, I saw my father shake his head in sincere confusion as he asked, "What happened to you, Esther? You used to be so sweet. You never used to backtalk me." I just mentally shook my head for I knew he didn't have a clue.

Why was our father so mean? He wasn't an alcoholic who would go on a binge and then mistreat us, for he rarely drank. Very few occasions did he come home tipsy from too many beers, and Mother was the only one who noticed. We children certainly saw no real difference in his behavior that indicated he had been drinking. I recall only one such time for there was definitely a difference in his behavior.

In the wee hours one morning, I awoke from a sound sleep when the front door slammed shut loudly. Then I heard Dad stumbling about noisily on his way to their bedroom, bumping into things, knocking chairs over. This surprised me for he usually came in very quietly after going out for the evening.

One time I asked Mom what "going out" meant when it was night time and what could Dad possibly do at night. She just shrugged and mumbled something about my father being "a ladies' man." She ignored my question as to what that term meant, and I never asked again.

So typically those nights when he finally did come home, he'd sneak in quietly, and later I'd hear arguing and then my mother's cries as she was beaten. But this time, things were different.

By the time I got to their bedroom, Dad had fallen on to the bed. Mother, in her gown, was tugging and rolling him over onto his back. He was obviously drunk but not passed out. Once she could see his face and force attention from his bleary eyes, Mom suddenly started yelling at him, beating him in the chest and shoulders with her small fists. She told him she didn't even know why she still loved him. He was just a no-good, cheating, wife-beating husband who, on top of that, was a rotten father who terrorized his poor children and was a lousy example of what a father should be—especially to his only son.

She had never talked to him like that before or raised a hand to him other than in self-defense or when he started to beat us for no reason when he was mad. I froze with terror expecting him to rise up and attack her. I was stunned, however, and slowly exhaled in shock when Dad started crying and agreeing with her, saying he was sorry. "You're right. I'm just no good," he whimpered. I couldn't believe my eyes and ears! Until that night, I'd never seen him docile or heard him say he was sorry about anything. I found myself wishing he'd drink more. That wish never came true, however, for I never saw him like that again.

More and more I found myself wondering why my mother married him and especially at such a young age. Very soon I would learn the answers, but they would only fuel my desire to do away with my father.

THE UNSUSPECTING BRIDE

One weekend following my fourteenth birthday, Mom and I were in the backyard trimming dead flowers from her prized bearded iris plants. The late afternoon sun highlighted their translucent petals, turning them into brilliant splashes of color. Deep purple, blue, amber, and bright golden hues filled the air with their sweet fragrance as a sudden playful breeze blew across the yard.

"Mom, why did you marry Dad when you were so young?" I asked, moving the bucket closer to her so she could deposit her pile of trimmings.

She didn't answer.

"Your mom and dad were great parents, and you got along well with your brothers and sister. I know you were poor because of Grandpa's crippled arm, and it must have been hard to go from place to place working crops, but you were happy. Why would you want to leave your parents and get married at the age of fourteen? I wouldn't dream of getting married now."

Still no answer.

"And why would Granny even let you?"

Mom straightened up from her bent position, leaned backward on her knees, rubbed her back, and began answering my questions.

"I was introduced to Clyde right after we moved to Oklahoma, and he started coming over and talking to me. He was a handsome, confident eighteen-year-old, and I was flattered. Here was this catch-of-the-town showing an interest in me, a shy girl who had barely turned fourteen."

"What do you mean 'catch-of-the-town'?"

"Well, that's what everybody called him. Besides, I'd seen how all the other girls hovered around him. Your granny told him he absolutely couldn't date me, said I was too young, but he kept coming over. He was very charming and relentless in his efforts to convince your granny that she should let us date. She finally told him he could go to church with us if he wanted to and he could sit next to me, but he still couldn't take me out alone on a date. Our family never missed a church service, and pretty soon, neither did Clyde."

"Well, if Granny wouldn't even let you date him at fourteen, how did you end up marrying him at that age?"

Mom fell silent. With furrowed brows, she sought the right words for her explanation. I snipped some dead blossoms from the plants further out into the bed and waited.

I heard Chuck and Chris laughing with their friends next door. *I love to hear them laugh,* I thought. *They certainly don't get to do a lot of that here. As much as we love each other, it seems like all we kids do is argue.* The thought bothered me, for I was older and felt I should set a better example. But I just couldn't help myself sometimes, and that made me feel even more irritable.

My legs were stiff. As I rose to stretch, a mockingbird flew over my head, loudly warning me not to venture near the Chinaberry tree where she nested.

"Mom?" I finally asked, picking up my snippers and kneeling again into the flowerbed.

"This may sound strange," she said, reaching for a tall iris, "but I didn't know I was getting married."

I whirled to face her, mouth open, eyes wide.

Before I could respond, she added, "That is, not until we all stood before the justice of the peace."

"You're kidding! How on earth could you not know you were getting married?"

We both rose to a sitting position. Mom smoothed her skirt out on the grass and said, "I didn't know it at the time, but Clyde had told your granny that he wanted to marry me. He said we were so madly in love that if she and your grandpa didn't sign for me and allow us to get married, then we would elope. He said he wasn't sure of where we would go next, nor when your granny and grandpa would see us again."

"You would do that? Just elope, not knowing if or when you'd see your parents again?"

"Of course not. As I said, I didn't know he had told Mom that."

"I don't understand. Why on earth would Granny let him bully her that way? She would stand up to the devil himself! And why would she agree to something as important as your marriage without even discussing it with you?"

"I guess your dad was so smooth and convincing—had all the plans made, even bought me a new dress, though it was much too big for me—that your granny assumed I was in on it and that was what I wanted. All of her lady neighbors had been raving about how great Clyde was, telling her, 'Mrs. Watson, that young Clyde sure would be a fine catch for little Esther. Handsome, hardworking, and everybody loves him. Why, any mother in this town would give her right arm to have him for a son-in-law'!"

"But you were so young!"

"Lots of teenage girls married back then and with their parents' blessings. I think the main reason your granny let me get married, though, was because your aunt Myrtie, my older sister, was giving them fits. She went through a sudden rebellious spell, just went wild—drinking, partying, staying out all night with disreputable guys."

Shocked, I exclaimed, "My aunt Myrtie did that? That doesn't sound like her!"

"Well, a lot of young people go through phases like that and are then sorry later. Of course, she isn't that way now. But it was during that time when my parents were totally distracted and beside themselves with worry about Myrtie that Clyde told them we were getting married in a week."

"But didn't Granny even talk with you about it?"

"It all happened so fast and so many things were going on—Myrtie's rebellion, them trying to work the crops. I think she assumed it was a done deal, so they just went along with it. And maybe deep inside, they thought I'd be safe if I married a nice young man. One thing I know for sure is that your granny has grieved herself almost sick ever since for letting me get married."

Poor Granny. How many times have I heard her say to me, "Till my dyin' day I'll never forgive myself for letting little Esther marry your father!" But how could she know he was such a rotten apple?

"So how did it happen? When did you finally realize you were getting married?"

"Well, it happened this way. Your dad gave me the new dress, which he'd said was okay with your granny for me to keep—only I didn't know it would be my wedding dress. He said it was for me to wear on a special occasion very soon, when we would take an all-day trip to Idabel, the county seat. He said he wanted me to wear it then to look pretty for him. In those days, wedding dresses were rarely the white, fluffy things girls wear now. It was hard times back then, and we had to be practical. So this had to fit any dress-up event such as for a party on Saturday night, church on Sunday, or going into a larger town, which was always special.

"I remember how excited I was when the following Saturday we all piled into your uncle Verdie's old Ford coupe, your dad and I sitting in the rumble seat, and drove to town. It was only when the county clerk started asking questions that I realized we were there for my wedding."

"Why didn't you say something?"

"By that time, I was absolutely nuts about your father, and I thought, *Well, I love him, so why not?*"

I couldn't believe what I was hearing. "Mom, I don't care how much you thought you loved him. Why would you marry someone who would deceive your parents and keep you in the dark about your own wedding? Especially someone so mean that he would knock you around?"

"At that time, I didn't know he had deceived them. And it suddenly all seemed very romantic to me. Like my knight in shining armor who chose me out of all the young maidens in the village and loved me so much that he'd surprise me this way and whisk me off into the sunset on his white horse. Besides, he never appeared mean. He was always mannerly and thoughtful to all of us. How could I know how he really was? Besides, I'd never seen any of the men in our families beat up their wives and children. Why would I think any man would do such a thing? I just figured we'd 'live happily ever after.'"

"So when was the first time he hit you?"

"We'd been married about a month. One day while your dad was gone, I was sweeping the wooden floor in our kitchen, happy to be a wife cleaning her own little place, when I noticed a loose board. With childlike curiosity, I lifted the end of it and peered below. It was dark down there, but when my eyes finally adjusted, I saw a number of bottles filled with brown-colored liquid lying in rows on the ground. I was really excited! This was a mystery, and I couldn't wait to share it with my new husband.

"As soon as he got home, I took him by the hand and danced him into the kitchen, saying 'I want to show you something.' I knelt over and eagerly pulled up the board. 'Look at what I found! What's in those bottles, and what do you think they're doing there'?

"Clyde didn't move. Just stared at me. His piercing blue eyes turned cold. Suddenly, he doubled up his fist and knocked me backwards onto the floor. I was horrified and confused. This was the man I loved and who loved me. Why was my knight, who was supposed to protect me, acting this way? My right jaw ached, already puffy. *Something is terribly wrong!* I thought. 'But what—,' I started to ask. Before I could get the words out, he hit me again. I started screaming and sobbing, and he just hit me harder.

"'Don't you ever ask me about those bottles again! And don't go telling anyone about them. This will teach you to not go poking your nose into things that are private, that are none of your business! If I want you to know something, I'll tell you.' Then he just walked out the front door and left me there in a huddle on the floor, bleeding and crying. As if he didn't even care."

I realized I had been holding my breath, mesmerized by the painful words falling from my mother's lips. I let out a long sad sigh. *What a horrible experience for a new little bride! And even worse, what a terrible way to learn that your husband is not the person you thought he was. My poor little mommy.*

"I'm so sorry," I said, the words catching in my throat as I reached out and pulled her close. Our tears mingled as we clung together.

The lump of pain was so large in my throat that I thought I would gag. Finally, when I could speak, I asked, "Why didn't you leave Dad once you found out what he was like? It would have been easier before we children were born."

Mom wiped the long raven strands of hair from the sides of her face, where they had been plastered by tears. Her cameo skin was flawless except for the remnants of a fading bruise on the lower right side of her face. *She is so beautiful! And so gentle. She looks like a queen, the same Queen Esther in the Bible she was named after. No wonder Dad picked her out of all the others.* My heart ached to think of all she had endured. Her large hazel eyes softened as they looked into mine.

"I didn't leave because I loved him. He wasn't mean to me all the time. You know, just like he isn't mean to us all the time now—even though he seems to be getting worse. Quite often he is pleasant, even jokes with us and takes us places. Remember that doll bed and furniture set he hand carved for you for Christmas when you were little? He worked so hard on it and painted it that perfect shade of blue that you like."

I remembered. I loved that set and treasured it for years. *Until he smashed it to pieces!*

"It's just that we don't know what's going to set him off or when. So we live in fear. Back then, he was more loving and did nice things for me, especially after he beat me up. I knew that it was only when I asked him about something that he didn't want me to know about or I did something he didn't like that he would beat me. At first, I didn't think I deserved to be treated that way, but as time went on, I thought if I would just try harder and be a better wife, he would outgrow what I thought was just a youthful temper."

"Isn't it strange how Dad is always trying to 'teach somebody something' by beating them up?" I interrupted. "I remember the story you told me of how when we lived in Fulton, Dad hit a man in the head with a pole ax, and he almost died. Dad accused him of stealing fish from the trotline he'd set out in the Red River. No wonder the poor man carried a gun for months afterward once he recovered! I still can't believe that judge only fined Dad $25 for disturbing the peace when he appeared in court. Disturbing the peace, my eye! That man would be dead had the other men not grabbed Dad's arms and held him."

"Yes, your father still brags about how lucky he was that the judge happened to have a grudge against the other man."

No wonder Dad thinks he can get away with anything—even murder.

"For your sake, Mom, I wish you could have left Dad before we kids were born. It's not that I have ever, for a minute, been sorry I was born. Even though life is scary and hurtful much of the time, I love being alive and am thankful that I exist. There is so much beauty in this world, beauty that you have taught me to appreciate, Mom. I shudder to think of missing out on life."

"You almost did," she said softly.

"What do you mean?"

"Your dad never really wanted a baby, said he didn't want the responsibility. Though one time he said it might be fun having a son to take fishing and hunting with him—and teach him how to be a man. But when I told him I was pregnant, he beat me up several times hoping I would abort you, but thank God I didn't. When you were a couple of years old, he got to thinking how he'd like a son. So when I got pregnant with Chuck, he didn't beat me, hoping for a boy. He was happy at having a son but said he didn't want any more kids. After that, every time I got pregnant, he beat me up so badly I miscarried."

Horrified, I didn't know what to say. I silently fought back tears.

Curiosity, our big yellow tabby, padded softly through the grass to Mom and let her know he wanted to be petted. Mom took the opportunity to get off her knees for a rest. Sitting down in the grass, she leaned against a garden bench, spread out her skirt, and let Ross, as we nicknamed him, crawl into her lap. He started kneading her belly and purring loudly as she gently stroked him.

Returning back to her sad memories, Mom continued, "It was so hard. For months following each miscarriage I cried—being careful to not do it when your dad was around as he'd get mad—because I never got to hold and love my precious baby. It hurt even more just knowing it had been killed by its own father."

I moved further over to trim some taller deep purple iris, almost black in color, so Mom couldn't see my tears. I sensed her need to verbalize her years of pent-up anguish now that I was old enough to understand, and I didn't want her to worry about overburdening me. I loved her with all of my heart and couldn't even imagine such emotional pain, not to mention the physical pain. Though she spoke without bitterness, as though she were relating a story she had read somewhere, the bitterness in my heart grew with each revelation.

"Thank God," she continued, "I carried your little sister until she was born."

Yes, thank you, Lord! I can't imagine life without adorable Chris and her perky personality.

"I lived in fear of getting pregnant again, but when I tried to explain that to your father, he wasn't cooperative. So when Chris was a toddler and I got pregnant, your dad was really upset. When none of his beatings resulted in a miscarriage, he made an appointment for me with an out-of-town doctor to get an abortion. I was absolutely terrified! I would have rather miscarried from a beating. I started shaking and trembling so bad while sitting there waiting my turn in the doctor's 'waiting room' in that ugly old house that needed painting, that I miscarried right there."

Speechless with shock at all the pain my young mother had gone through, I could only stare in disbelief. To ease the suffocating ache in my throat, I looked away as tears trickled down my face.

"As I look back," she said reflectively, "I believe it was a blessing that I got that infection and ended up having a hysterectomy. I never had to worry about getting pregnant again and losing precious babies."

I stood up and stretched, suddenly thirsty. "Mom, why don't you relax while I go in and get us some ice cold lemonade." I didn't dare look at her as I hurried into the house.

Although the fresh lemonade felt good on my parched throat, I frowned and shuddered. *Definitely needs to be sweeter!* I spooned extra sugar into both glasses as well as the pitcher, stirring both with a long-handled wooden spoon. Somehow, I was cheered by the tinkling sound made when I stirred the mixture of ice water, lemon slices, and ice chips.

After placing the tray on the bench behind Mom, I handed her the other glass. After taking a long swallow, Mom continued. "I really did try to get away from your father, honey."

Puzzled, I asked "What do you mean 'try'? Either you did or you didn't."

"Those bottles that I saw under the kitchen floor that day were filled with illegal whiskey. Your daddy's mother had set him and his older and younger brothers up in an illegal moonshine business. As you know, their mom was the sole support of her family following the mysterious death of your dad's father when he was only three. Oklahoma was a dry state, and their still produced enough corn liquor to supply most of the county, including many in the local sheriff's department and the local bawdy house."

Shocked, I said, "The sheriff's department? But that's illegal! How could anyone feel safe with those who were hired to protect them breaking the law themselves?"

"Honey, I'm sure the entire department wasn't involved, just several of your dad's cronies. There's bound to be rotten apples in every barrel, you know."

My thoughts returned to her reference about my paternal grandfather's death. I had often wondered how he died, but Mom had warned us to never ask, saying the price of our curiosity could be costly.

There was a mystery about Dad's side of the family that intrigued me. There seemed to be tons of relatives on my mother's side of the family—so many cousins that I'd not even met them all. But not on my father's side. Dad's family appeared to consist of only his two brothers, their wives and children, and Dad's mom—and her succession of either husbands or live-ins. *Dad has to have other relatives,* I often thought. *But why won't he talk about them?*

As always, when the truth is missing, there is a proliferation of rumors. From one paternal cousin, we heard that Dad's grandfather had been hanged as a horse thief. From another, it was rumored that my father had been named after the infamous Clyde Barrow, who was a distant renegade uncle of some sorts. I grew up believing that rumor until I was grown and through research learned Clyde Barrow was born only ten years before my dad's birth.

"So, when did you try to leave Dad? And what prevented you?"

"I'm getting to that part. My mother found out about the illegal still while I was carrying you. Your dad didn't want to be bothered with me because I was extremely sick during my pregnancy, so he dumped me on your granny and grandpa. They were thrilled to have me with them, where they knew you and I would be safe away from your father's beatings.

"Clyde did pride himself, however, on being a responsible person when it came to paying his debts. Just as he still does. Before you were to be born, he paid a local doctor in advance to deliver you. He then left on a hunting trip feeling pretty good about himself. We learned later that the doctor's medical license had been revoked for drunken malpractice. Since Clyde had paid him in a case of moonshine, the 'doctor' showed up drunk. Your granny assisted him, but when he started to yank your umbilical cord out instead of cutting it, she pushed him aside and forced him to leave. Grabbing some scissors, she cut the cord herself and finished taking care of both of us. Had she not taken over, who knows what might have happened."

I involuntarily shuddered at the thought and again ached for my little mommy.

"Immediately after you were born, your granny called the revenuers, who came and destroyed the still. Your dad and his older brother were sent to prison for a year, but their youngest brother didn't have to go since he was so young.

"You and I stayed at home with my folks while your father was in prison. I was worried sick, but thank goodness, nobody ever learned your granny was the one who called the feds. I decided that I was going to leave your father after he got out of prison. When he finally showed up, I was scared to death, but somehow I got the courage to tell him I wanted a divorce."

My pulse quickened as I imagined the scene.

"What did Dad say?"

"Nothing. He was quiet for a minute and just grinned that evil grin of his. 'That's okay, honey,' he finally said with a sneer. 'You can have a divorce, but I'm keeping the baby.'

"I was surprised and wondered why he now all of a sudden wanted the responsibility of a baby when I knew how well he liked the ladies. When I objected, he just laughed and said, 'I have friends in the sheriff's department who owe me favors. They'll swear that you are an unfit mother, that you slept with them all the time I was gone, and believe me, I *will* get the baby. So go ahead and divorce me if you want to.' Then he leaned back in his chair and laughed."

I can just see him! I didn't think it was possible for me to hate him any more, but now I do! I thought. My next realization, however, quickly turned my anger into guilt. *Oh, my! It was Mom's love for me, her precious baby that held her as Dad's captive. Had it not been for me she would be free. I've got to do something to help! But what?*

My mind raced toward the thoughts I had been entertaining for weeks. Now they were doubly fueled. *I will not let Dad keep on winning! The next time he starts beating Mom and threatening us with his gun, I will get it somehow and I will shoot him! So help me, God!*

THE BITTER FRUITS OF FRUSTRATION

The pressure swelled within me. I knew I had to do something— but shoot my own father? Could I deliberately aim the gun at him and pull the trigger? *I've got to look for another way out.* For several months I considered various options.

I could try to convince our mother to take us children and leave. That was a most unlikely option. At that time our nation hadn't yet addressed the issue of domestic violence. There were no shelters or aid of any kind available. Our only hope was to be taken in by relatives, but that presented greater problems. We knew that if we fled to sympathetic relatives for refuge, our father would find us, and their lives as well as ours would be endangered.

I could call the police and have my father arrested. From experience, I knew that option would be an exercise in futility. When I was eleven years old, I had tried that. This particular night Dad was beating Mother so badly I feared she would die. While Chuck and Chris trembled in their rooms at the far end of the house, I slipped out the back door and called the police from our neighbor's house. I crept back into my room and waited in the darkness for them to arrive. I was certain Dad would be arrested, put in jail, and we'd be safe forever.

Heart pounding, I watched from my bedroom window as two tall policemen walked up onto our front porch. I heard Dad hissing instructions and threats at Mom from their bedroom across the hall about how she should talk to them. After responding to their forceful knocks, she opened the front door but spoke to them only through the screen. They could still see her ripped gown, bruises, and bleeding head revealed in the glare of the yellow porch light. When they asked her about it, she said she had slipped and fallen. After a long conversation with Mom, my relief at their arrival changed to horror when I realized my heroes were going to leave without my father. Despite their concern, they could do nothing because our frightened mother refused to press charges.

Suddenly, I was terrified! I feared Dad would kill me if he learned it was I who called the police. I burst from my room, pushed open the screen door just as the officers were turning to leave. Desperate, I grabbed one of them around the leg and held on so he couldn't move without dragging me. Sobbing, I begged "Please take me with you! I'm afraid—I don't want to live here anymore!" For the first time I thought only of my safety.

Even in my terror, I was touched by the sadness I saw in that officer's eyes as he gently disengaged me and explained they couldn't take me with them. They walked me back as my shocked mom opened the door. But I dashed past her arms to my room and hid under my bed covers. After again talking with Mom for some time, the officers slowly walked back to their patrol car. I peeked out my window, still trembling, and watched them standing there talking for some time before slowly driving away. I stiffened with fear that Dad would now come after me, but I didn't hear any more sounds after Mom returned to their bedroom.

Thankfully, Dad never learned it was I who called the police. Our neighbors never mentioned anything about that night and simply ignored everything that happened at our house. But it was several weeks before our Dad hit Mom again.

I could run away from home. I could just leave, but I feared that my newfound freedom might lead to a worse prison. I had heard horrible stories about runaways. I feared I might become another child of the street—one of the many who are sucked into oblivion through crime, addiction, or prostitution, since I wouldn't be able to adequately support myself. And yet, didn't I deserve a chance at life? What hope did I have at home? Nothing there was going to change, except get worse. If I left, I might be a lucky runaway.

I could marry as early as possible. I seriously considered this, but seeing firsthand the negative results of a teen marriage, I definitely didn't want to repeat my mother's mistake. Because Mom married when she was fourteen and I was born when she was fifteen, she was forced to stay in her abusive marriage. If I followed in her footsteps, I would be destined to repeat history, and the cycle of abuse would likely continue. But didn't I deserve a chance for happiness? Maybe a better candidate than my dad would come along, and my marriage might be a good one.

I could remain at home. My home situation would not likely improve, but by staying, I could at least give my siblings and mother my love and moral support. I also would not expose myself to worse unknown dangers. While providing no quick fix for my pain, this choice might be my best, considering my list of poor options. But to stay home and remain miserable seemed unthinkable.

I could eliminate the source of my problem. From time to time, I heard or read about individuals who were acquitted for shooting someone in self-defense. *Maybe I wouldn't be convicted either,* I thought. *Surely the courts would understand that I was only defending my family.* But what if I were convicted? I feared I couldn't handle prison. And yet, wasn't there a chance I might be acquitted?

I could commit suicide. I was a likely candidate. Not only was I unhappy and afraid, I was tired of my heavy burden of responsibility. And those recurring dreams of helplessness were getting worse. I fought frequent bouts of depression and carried the added weight of low self-esteem. And I was a failure. It was obvious I couldn't protect or rescue my mom and siblings. And if we were to somehow escape from Dad, how would I provide for them? I believed my father when he told me I was ugly and stupid and that I would never amount to anything. If I was so worthless that even my own father recognized it, what hope did I have for a happy future? Life just didn't seem to offer much.

Which option should I choose? Did I really have a choice, or was I just a pawn in the game of life?

A CHOICE IS MADE

One day I read a newspaper article that reported the acquittal of a teenage boy who had shot and killed his father during an attack upon the mother.

Good for him! I thought. *That father got exactly what he deserved.* I laid the paper down, but I couldn't get the article out of my mind. *Surely a jury wouldn't convict me either for defending my family if I shot my father. But even if it did, so what? At least Mom and the kids would be free.*

But each time I imagined how I might grab the gun from him, I was plagued by fears. *What if during his next attack I can't get the gun? If I am able to wrestle it from him, can I really force myself to take aim at him and deliberately pull the trigger? What if I attempt and fail? He'll kill us all!*

But my greatest fear was that I might succeed.

I was so tenderhearted; it pained me to see a dead mouse in a trap. I rescued countless injured birds that had fallen from their nests and took them to the loving hands of my mother, who, after nursing them to health, set them free. For years, I grieved after Dad's sleep was disturbed one night by the whining of our family dog's puppies, he brutally killed them. Following a search the next morning, I stumbled upon their bloody bodies strewn among the weeds on the back of our property.

What is the matter with me? It hurts me to see a dead animal; how can I even think of killing my own father, no matter how terrible he is? But I am my family's only hope, I argued. *If I don't do something, who will?*

One night, my heart cried out to a God I had heard about from Granny—but I wasn't even sure he actually existed. Granny seemed to have a lot of faith in Him. Yet, it wasn't like I had anyone else to pray to—besides, I was desperate. *God, if you're as powerful as Granny says,* I prayed, *then why don't you do something? Why do you allow my dad to be so mean to us?*

From the depths of my anguished soul, I pleaded, *If you really do exist, please help me. I didn't ask to be born into this situation. I'm supposed to do something, but I don't know what. When Chuck and Chris are terrified as Mom is being beaten, I try to keep them quiet so Dad won't get more upset. I tell them that everything will be okay, but I know it won't. After Dad leaves and slams the door, I hold Mom close and tell her how sorry I am that she is hurt. I can't fix this problem, God. It's too big, and I'm too small. But if you won't do something, I guess I'll have to.*

I wept bitter tears into my pillow and decided, *God's not real, anyway. How could he care?* At an age when most teenagers look forward to a happy future with joyful anticipation, I waited for my dad's next attack—the perfect provocation for me to shoot him.

A NEW DIRECTION

One Sunday afternoon shortly after my prayer, Mom's youngest brother, Uncle Paul, stopped by and asked, "Kitty, would you like to go to church with your aunt Ruth and me this evening?"

"I don't think Dad will let me—he says religion is a crutch for weaklings," I answered. "But I'd like to."

"Why don't you ask him? He might." For some strange reason, I found myself really wanting to go, pleading silently as I went to ask permission. *God, if religion is just a crutch, then I must qualify, because I feel like I'm falling apart. I really need something to lean on.*

Surprisingly, Dad let me go.

I sat spellbound by the message I heard that night. The minister spoke of how each of us lives under the penalty of death. He said that we are hopelessly and helplessly trapped as prisoners in a world that is terminally polluted with sin—sin that resulted from Adam and Eve's wrong choice in the garden of Eden. He then spoke of a loving God who provided a way for us to escape—a way that offered freedom instead of bondage, victory instead of defeat, and love instead of hate.

I longed for freedom and how I craved the love of a father! *But how could God love me?* I wondered. *I don't deserve any of these good things since I am so worthless. My earthly father doesn't love me, how can I expect a perfect God to love me? Especially since I have these evil thoughts in my heart.*

But the speaker stressed the heavenly Father's love, his goodness, and how he could be trusted to keep his word. He held up his tattered black Bible and read from it John 3:16 "For God so loved the world that he gave his only Son, so that everyone who believes in him will not perish but have eternal life."

As the minister spoke, a strange thing happened. He suddenly stopped and, pointing his finger, it seemed as though straight at me, declared in a loud voice, "And 'whosoever' has to include you, because God is not a liar!"

I was stunned. *It must be true,* I reasoned. *A God this loving wouldn't deliberately leave someone out, so his invitation has to include me!*

The best part was it didn't matter that I didn't deserve it, for he went on to explain that God's love and forgiveness is a gift. Through Christ, his Son, God was offering love, not judgment; forgiveness, not condemnation. He offered life because he had conquered death through the cross and resurrection. I didn't understand all that I heard, but a tiny spark of hope began to glimmer.

I had no time to go on a worldwide theological search for spiritual truths. Time was running out, and I had to make a decision. *I can choose to pursue the path to kill my father,* I thought, *or I can choose the door opening before me and trust God with my life.*

As I weighed my choices, the minister explained that to accept God, I had to interact with him in a personal way. "You don't just try to keep a set of rules in hopes of impressing God into loving you, God already loves you. You can't do one thing to cause Him to love you any more than he already does."

Then he added, "All of the great religions of the world tell us that we should to try to reach God by living good and honest lives, loving our enemies, and forgiving those who wrong us. Their books tell us what we should do, but they don't tell us *how* to do it. They just give us more rules.

"Christianity, based on the Holy Bible, is different," he explained. It's not a religion. Sadly, some Christians, though, treat it like it is by merely counting how many times they go to church and how much money they give. But that's the same as keeping more rules. Becoming a Christian is all about having a relationship with the one and only living God, a God who doesn't ask us to try hard to reach him through our feeble efforts—he knows we can't. It is through Christ that God reaches down to us on our level, right where we are, regardless of our condition, and invites us to Him.

"You see," he went on, "we are changed *after* we accept Christ, for it is only then that we have the power to become all that God created us to be. Not before."

My mind raced with excitement. *If I don't have to clean up my act in order to be accepted by God, then maybe there is a chance for me. This is my only hope!* I decided, bowing my head. From the depths of my soul came the admission. *I need You, God. I want you in my life. It's hard for me to believe that all of these things could be true, but I don't have anywhere else to go. Please forgive me and help me to become what you want me to be.*

It was actually more of a pleading than anything, for I could not put into words the needs of my soul. But it didn't matter. God, who hears the faintest cry of the weakest heart, heard mine and answered its longings. Very softly and gently, his love entered my heart and life, and a miracle took place. The heavy burden I had carried all of my life was lifted, and I was free!

Though the choice I made that evening would impact my life forever (and for all eternity), it did not come with a free pass from pain. And the pain I had experienced before was nothing compared to what lay ahead!

SO WHERE ARE THE ROSES?

God never promised us a rose garden. He did promise us, however, strength and power to function within a bitter and thorny environment.

> Sometimes, God doesn't change our circumstances; he changes us in our circumstances.
>
> —Carla Killough McClafferty, *Forgiving God*

I returned home that night to the same circumstances, the same danger, and the same heartaches. Nothing there had changed. But I had. Through Christ, I was a new person, a child of God whom he had promised to love and strengthen. I didn't know then how much I would need God's love and strength, for the situation at home not only didn't improve, it worsened. But for the moment I had a breather. A lull before the storm.

Dad allowed me to attend church only a few times after that, but I prayed and studied the Bible the pastor gave me. I grew stronger, and my attitude began to change, but I needed to be with other Christians. There was so much in the Bible I didn't understand. I had so many questions but there was no one to ask. Granny could have answered them, but she lived too far away. Uncle Paul and Aunt Ruth moved out of town, and I had no way to attend church, even if Dad had let me.

Lord, I really need to go to church. I'm getting depressed again, and I feel like I'm fighting a losing battle with my flare-ups of hate.

When I was sixteen, some young people invited me to their church, and to my surprise, Dad let me attend. Shortly afterwards, I joined the church and was baptized. Although I still couldn't attend as often as I wanted, I was allowed to go on Sunday mornings. I began to blossom spiritually as I was nurtured in the loving atmosphere of the church and other Christians.

I found the more I responded to God's Word and tried to live by it, the stronger I grew. Anger still flared, as was natural, especially during Dad's brutal outbursts, but it didn't consume me.

Though my father's episodes seemed to be lessening in frequency, I noticed a new subtlety on his part. After beating my mother, he would often verbalize his reasons. "Your mother nags me too much." "I've had a bad day." Or, "It's because you kids upset me." There was always some excuse.

What's with his excuses? I wondered. *He never bothered to rationalize his abuse before.* I suspected he longed for the younger ones' affection and didn't want them to be afraid of him. I was sure he felt it was too late to fool me, for I had seen too much of his brutality, but he might be able to convince Chuck and Chris that he wasn't responsible for his actions.

Something else bothered me. His violent episodes appeared to coincide with the times I was gone, and this became an added burden for me. As a teenager, I needed outside activities, but because I felt responsible for the family's safety, I worried all the time I was gone. Other times, I stayed away longer, dreading to come home. Then I felt guilty for being so selfish. These conflicting emotions resulted in unexpected bursts of hate and resentment that I feared would destroy me. One night I lost control. Shaking, with fists clenched, I yelled at my father, "I hate you! I hope you rot in your grave!" As I turned to walk away, Dad doubled up his fist and hit me on the side of my head so hard I almost passed out. Not only did I suffer physically from that outburst, but I was filled with shame and remorse at having failed my Lord with such un-Christian-like behavior. Many nights I fell into a fitful sleep, praying, "Lord, I know I'm supposed to pray for my enemies, but it's hard when the enemy is my own father."

One night just before graduation, I returned home from a church service to find Dad beating Mom with his gun. I remember it clearly—it was a Colt .45 on a .38 frame. *Oh, no, Lord! What triggered him this time?* I ran to Mother's side and pushed myself between them.

Suddenly I felt the cold steel muzzle of his gun jam hard into my temple. My heart raced, pounding wildly against the Bible I clutched close to my chest.

"One of these days I'm going to blow your head off. I'm sick and tired of your interfering," my father said evenly, without emotion. His steel blue eyes bored into mine.

Suddenly, an inner voice from deep within me said, *Now is your chance. Why don't you just wrestle the gun from his hand and shoot him? He isn't getting any better, he's only getting worse. Things will never change. Just grab the gun and get it over with.*

I stood still, barely breathing. The thoughts continued, seductive in their rationale. *Surely God would understand. After all, how much does he expect you to endure? Why don't you just do what you planned to do years ago?*

Suddenly, I recalled some words I had recently read, "Don't be afraid of those who want to kill you. They can only kill your body; they cannot touch your soul. Fear only God, who can destroy both your soul and your body in hell" (Matthew 10:28), and "Don't be afraid, for I am with you. Do not be dismayed, for I am your God. I will strengthen you. I will help you. I will uphold you with my victorious right hand" (Isaiah 41:10).

The tempter's voice sneered, *Yeah, just like he's helping you right now, with a gun pointed to your head! That's helping?*

Just as a doubt began to take form, another scripture suddenly sprang to mind: "'For I know the plans I have for you,' says the

Lord. 'They are plans for good and not for disaster, to give you a future and a hope'" (Jeremiah 29:11). *Please help me, Lord! I want to believe your words and trust this situation to you!*

Staring unflinchingly into the eyes of my father, I said softly, "If that's what you want to do, Dad, go ahead and pull the trigger. I'm ready to die. I'll just go to heaven and be where you can't hurt me anymore. But remember this, someday you will stand before God and be held accountable for your actions." I said this firmly but with respect.

He saw no fear in my eyes, but for the first time I saw a glimmer of what looked like fear in his. He lowered the gun and never again threatened me in that way.

On graduation night I numbly walked across the stage and accepted my diploma. For years, Mom had looked forward to my high school graduation ceremony, but my dad had beaten her so badly she couldn't attend. Chuck, my only family supporter in attendance, gave me a hug before we quickly left. I couldn't bear to stay and watch the happy families around me.

But even worse pain was yet to come.

THE ESCAPE

The fall following my high school graduation, I began my first full-time job as a secretary at Highland Park Elementary School near our home. I loved the students and adored the principal, a petite, dynamic woman just under five feet tall. Mrs. Latona Watts commanded loving respect from everyone, even children taller than she. She endeared herself to me quickly with her caring and perky personality. And she made me laugh.

Sometimes she'd put her arm around my shoulder and guide me to a corner, where she whispered confidentially, as though she were divulging a high military secret, "Kitty, people are *strange*. They'll give you a dollar and fall out with you over a nickel!"

From time to time her little granddaughter, who attended our school, would spend the night with Latona. Because she had to be at school early to open up, it was left to Latona's husband Tom to feed their granddaughter, dress her, and get her off to school on time. They lived just a short walking distance from school so their granddaughter was never late. Sometimes Tom would amble into our office around midmorning, and Latona would chew him out royally!

With hands on her hips, she glared up at her good-natured husband who stood a good head and shoulders above her, and demanded "Tom Watts, how could you not notice that that poor little thing's socks don't match?"

Tom would shrug, make some kind of excuse, and they'd go back and forth until Latona got tired, turned off her hearing aid, and yelled, "You may as well go home, Tom Watts—I can't hear a word you're saying!"

I loved their antics for they never seemed to be really mad and it was obvious they loved and respected each other dearly. Something I wasn't used to seeing.

That first year was wonderful. Though we continued to tip-toe around our volcano at home, there weren't too many violent eruptions. I began dating the local junior high football coach, and life was good—as good as it could be. But not for long.

Very early one morning, several days before my nineteenth birthday, Dad began beating Mother, and I intervened. Pushing myself between him and Mom, I asked softly, "Dad, if you are so miserable with us, why don't you just leave?"

"No one will ever make me leave my house! You leave," he snarled and punched me in the face. Mom lunged for the phone. For the first time, she called the police. She wouldn't tolerate that kind of treatment to us kids. After knocking me to the floor, Dad tried to wrestle the phone from her, but not before her screams for the police were heard by the operator.

A LINE IS DRAWN

This time Mother planned to press charges. She had drawn a line in the sand, regardless of the consequences, for life or death; we could no longer live this way.

The officers came, handcuffed Dad, and took him to jail. Our hearts pounded as we rushed to the courthouse. We had been instructed to be there at 8:30 a.m. if we wanted to press formal charges. *Maybe this is the beginning of our freedom,* I hoped. But hope turned to horror when we arrived shortly after eight and learned that Dad had been released. The one who had threatened to kill us if we ever reported him now waited for us at home.

My heart raced, and my palms were sticky. I opened my mouth, but there was nothing I could say in response to the clerk. I whirled around, facing Mom and the children. Mom's shoulders suddenly sagged. Her eyes, wide in terror, stared at me like a frightened fawn as her face crumpled. Chris began sobbing silently as she buried her face into Mom's arm, clinging to her.

Chuck's pale face showed no emotion, but his fists were doubled at his sides.

My mind, foggy with fear, went blank. What could I do for our little family? The line that Mom had so courageously drawn was now full circle, and we were trapped within it. *Lord, what can we do?*

We couldn't go to neighbors. Nor could we go to Granny's house. Not only was it hours away, it was one of the first places he would look. There was no way out. We were doomed.

Suddenly the fog cleared. *The church! That's the only safe place.*

I herded everyone into the car and then drove quickly to the church. Dr. Hope, our pastor, sat stunned as we explained our situation. He listened to us and prayed with us. He never left our side. He drove us to the courthouse, where assault and battery charges of a minor were filed against Dad. The pastor recommended an attorney and then drove us to his office, where Mom filed for a divorce. We stayed at the church most of that day where we felt safe and secure.

Mom called a next-door neighbor and apprised her of the situation. "I saw the police car," Mrs. Shaw said, "when they brought Clyde back to the house. Then later, I saw the police car return and take him away again in handcuffs."

We breathed easier and felt it was safe for us to return home. At least for a while.

Dad had time to think in jail and to assess his situation. He was in a tough spot. His private treatment of us was now on public record. He knew that Mother would have no problem getting a divorce. She would likely be awarded the house along with monthly child support. His plan to use temporary insanity as a plea for killing us was less plausible than ever.

Three months prior to this, Mom had made her decision to accept Christ as her personal Savior and had been baptized. Dad had noticed a change in her, just as he had noticed the change in me following my spiritual choice years earlier.

Now it was his turn to make a spiritual decision. But there was one major difference: behind his "decision" lay an ulterior motive. He most likely recalled a statement Mom had made that if ever they were separated, the only way she would take him back was if he were a new person spiritually.

Dad called Dr. Hope and asked him and some of the church deacons to come and pray with him, saying he wanted to become a Christian. They went, talked with him, prayed with him, and read Scriptures. After a long discussion, Dad prayed a wonderful "prayer of repentance."

As a result of his "conversion," we dropped all charges, and Dad returned home. He went before the church, gave a splashy testimony as to how he had been changed by God, and this charismatic new convert was baptized. The church rejoiced, for a sinner had come home.

And indeed he had! Two weeks later, he was beating Mom again. We were more miserable than ever. We knew we'd been conned, as had the church. Only the church didn't know it—yet.

Shortly afterwards, we were on an Independence Day outing at a rural public park. Dad and Mom had gone for a walk in a densely-wooded area while we young people played games. Suddenly, piercing screams shattered the happy chatter and sounds of the peaceful afternoon. Everyone stopped and looked toward the woods. My heart froze for I knew it was our mother. Several people joined us as we ran toward the screams.

Suddenly, Mother emerged from the trees, running and stumbling, blood streaming down her face. As we reached her, she gasped out her story of how Dad had become angry and beaten her on the side of the head with a rock. The crowd grew, staring in confusion and shock as I tried to stop the bleeding from Mom's head with a scarf and wipe the blood from her face with napkins someone handed me. Dad quickly strode into view.

His handsome face broke into a broad smile, his blue eyes crinkled in understanding as he explained, "She is hysterical, poor little thing. Fell and hit her head on a rock, became disoriented, and panicked. She just started screaming and running."

Reaching down to help her, he chuckled softly, adding, "Boy, can people run fast when they panic!"

Visible relief spread across the faces of some of the men nearest us when Dad gently lifted Mom up by the waist and said sweetly, "Here, sweetheart, it's okay."

"I did not slip and fall," Mother tried to interject. But Dad just talked soothingly over her objections. "Here, here, I understand, honey, you've had a nasty fall, but everything's going to be okay when we get you home."

Understandably, believing my father's story relieved the onlookers of any responsibility in this situation. Besides, what could they do? But we children knew the truth, and it wasn't okay. A sense of urgency pounded within me. *We have to get away from him soon, but how?*

Several days later, Mom asked Dad if she could take us children and go to visit her sister in San Francisco for a few weeks. She tried to convince him that once she was rested up and had recuperated, she'd probably feel a lot better about everything.

Dad was quiet for a moment, mentally chewing on the idea. Finally, he agreed but said we children had to remain. Mom blanched and looked out the window, brows knitted in deep concentration. I thought she was going to change her mind, but she said, "Okay."

Our home wasn't the same without our good-natured and cheery mother, but we were relieved that she was safe away from Dad. For the moment. We didn't know of her plans to stay longer than she had told our dad nor that she was forming a plan of escape.

One evening the phone rang in the living room and Dad answered. He talked for a while then hung up. "That was your mom," he announced. I thought it was strange because she always wanted to talk with me, check on the kids and see how we were doing.

Chuck and Chris had now joined me, waiting to hear what Dad was saying. Dad looked at each of us, making sure he had our attention, and said, "Your mother told me she has decided to stay in California. She's had time to think things over. She says it's fun not having to worry about a family so she's going to stay there—get on with her life."

Then as though he were giving a weather report, he added, "She said she doesn't love you kids anymore." Then he turned and walked out of the room.

Chris began to cry, and Chuck's face crumpled. I whispered as Dad left the room, "Don't believe a word of what he says—he's lying! Mother does love us—she would never leave us!"

We learned later that Dad had often called Mom, telling her to stay in California, stating we children didn't love her, that we would be happier without her, and that if she knew what was good for her, she wouldn't return home.

THE DECISION: GO OR STAY?

Two weeks later, I began my second year as school secretary. There was much to do to prepare for the onslaught of excited school children, but Mrs. Watts and I somehow accomplished it. Early in the morning, the second day after school started, the school phone rang. It was my mother. Thinking she was still in California, I said excitedly, "Hi, Mom!" But something was strange. She was whispering.

"Kitty, I'm home. Your aunt Myrtie and cousin Abner drove me here and will help us go back to California. This is our only chance to get away from your dad. Check Chris out of her classroom there, drive to Chuck's school, check him out, and come home immediately. I'm already packing."

Stunned, I cradled the phone in its stand. Mrs. Watts stared at my pale face. "What's wrong?" Even as I explained to her what was happening, I struggled within. Mrs. Watts was one of the few people who knew about my home situation. She was also one of the few who knew the real cause of the bruises that sometimes appeared on my face. She often hugged me, telling me she loved me like her own daughter. I loved working there with her. I loved the children. It broke my heart to think of leaving.

Suddenly, I was aware of someone calling my name.

"Kitty, listen to me," Mrs. Watts pled. "Please don't go. You're too young to have such a responsibility. You can stay with me. Besides, you can't help them anymore. Maybe your father will see that it's all over once they're in California, and he won't follow them. He'll just give up." Love glowed in her tear-filled eyes as Mrs. Watts took me by the shoulders and shook me gently. "You deserve a chance to be happy, so stay and live your own life. We'll get legal help to see that your father doesn't bother you. Don't go."

Suddenly, I stood at a crossroads that required another important choice. Should I leave or stay? I had grown very fond of Jim, the coach I was dating. There were definite romantic possibilities. He was a strong but gentle young man who cared for me deeply. I felt secure with him. I loved Mrs. Watts, and I loved my job, especially the children there. How could I leave them all so abruptly, without warning or explanation?

But how would Mom, Chuck, and Chris make it without me? They couldn't support themselves. Mom, with only a fourth-grade education, didn't even know how to drive. Dad would surely find them, and I wouldn't be there to protect them. If I stayed, I knew Dad would find me. Not only would my life be in danger but also the lives of anyone who helped me. What was I to do? Fierce pain pierced my heart as it was yanked in opposite directions.

Lord, I pleaded inwardly, *please help me. I don't know what to do. I don't have time to reason out all the advantages and disadvantages of my options.*

The room wasn't cold, but I started shaking. Somewhere in the deep recesses of my storm-tossed mind, icy winds of confusion whirled in darkness, chilling me to the core. I stood there, frozen in the cold reality of my emotional turbulence. From somewhere, a soft light formed a tiny spot deep within the center of my soul—a warm, calm, and quiet spot that seemed to pulsate as it enlarged. Its center revealed the choice I must make.

"I'm so sorry, Mrs. Watts," I stammered. "I must go. Please forgive me for leaving you at a time when you need me the most. How will you find a replacement on such short notice? And then there's Jim. It will break his heart that I left without saying good-bye. Would you please explain everything to him? I can't let anyone know where we are going. Not even you. We can't let my father find us!" (I hated causing anyone pain and would have felt better had I known that a year later Jim would marry a beautiful debutante. I rejoiced when I later heard the news because I cared deeply for Jim as a friend. He was a kind man who deserved happiness.)

Mrs. Watts lifted her head, and holding it high in determination, said, "Don't worry, I will take care of everything." Her breath caught as she gave me a long, hard hug and said, "I understand why you have to do what you are doing. I love you. You will be in my prayers constantly."

Heart pounding, I gathered up Chris and Chuck and rushed home.

Everything was in chaos there. Mother and Aunt Myrtie were tossing things into bags while Cousin Abner pushed items into the trunk of my aunt's car. Comprehension of the scene around me paralyzed me with fear. *What if Dad catches us as we are trying to leave? I glanced fearfully at the driveway. Why can't I think clearly? How do I choose what to take from all of my possessions when space is so limited?*

"Kitty, grab your things and put them into these pillowcases," Mom commanded, tossing them to me. "They will pack easier. Put them in our car trunk, your aunt's is almost full." After poking as much as we could into every available space, we jumped into the two cars and sped off, pursued only by our terror.

"Head for Granny's house," Mom said. "We've got to take her with us. That's the first place your dad will look, and she'll be in danger." Mom felt Dad was no threat to our step-grandpa.

After the two-hour trip to Hatfield, Arkansas, we picked up Granny and headed straight for California. Fear pushed us farther and faster with every mile. I looked in the rear-view mirror constantly, expecting to see my dad barreling down upon us. Other than for gas and quick pit stops and bites to eat, we fled nonstop to Needles, California, where we collapsed in a motel.

UNCLE JOHN'S HOUSE

The next morning we drove to Delhi, California, to my great uncle John's tiny house, where we were welcomed with open and loving arms. We had never met Uncle John, but we quickly fell in love with this man whose heart was twice as big as the meager abode he lovingly shared with us. We thanked God that he wholeheartedly sheltered our bedraggled, frightened family, quite possibly at the risk of his own life. Though we slept on pallets and our quarters were cramped, we were happy because we were free. At least for a while. Uncle John was Granny's oldest brother, a widower with an irresistible sense of humor.

"Honey," he said, holding up a can of beans our first evening there, "don't ever eat pork and beans!"

"Why not?" I asked, wide-eyed.

"Because you'll go blind."

"Why would eating pork and beans cause me to go blind?" I asked, walking perfectly into his trap.

"Because," he answered, eyes twinkling, "you'll go blind looking for the pork."

He then showed us two square little boards, which he described as ant killers. "How on earth can those little boards kill ants?" I asked.

"I'll show you," he said, picking up a board.

"You take an ant, place him on this here board like this. Then you take the other board and whack him real hard. Kills the ant every time."

He cooked cornbread in a big iron skillet, serving up thick slices with glasses of cold milk. We felt right at home.

I put in applications everywhere for secretarial work, and we did whatever we could to help put food on the table. We picked up walnuts and harvested grapes in the local vineyards. For a time, I worked at an almond-processing plant. Three elderly ladies and I sat in front of two conveyor belts where we sorted the almond nutmeats from the shells coming toward us on one belt and tossed them onto the other belt. I sat at the head of the assembly line and was the first one for the cracked almonds to reach. The women were pleasant, and I enjoyed their light-hearted conversation. I was quick and worked hard, but soon the job became boring. My only challenge was to see how fast I could work.

"Child, you should slow down a little. You're working too hard," the lady next to me cautioned.

The other two ladies chimed in and agreed.

I replied, with a quick toss of my long blond hair, "Oh, I don't mind," and reached in front of her for a missed nutmeat. "I like working hard. It makes the time go by faster."

Then the foreman cautioned me to slow down. "You don't have to work so hard, Kitty. There are three other ladies."

Pleased by all of this kind attention, I only worked faster. "I can't believe how nice everyone is there," I announced to everyone during supper one evening. "They actually worry about me working too hard!"

Thus, I was devastated when I received a "pink slip" with my next paycheck. Fighting back tears, I stammered "But why? I've been a hard worker." *Besides, I really need this job!* I screamed inside. The foreman just shrugged and thanked me for the time I had worked there. Later, I put the clues together and figured out why. The other ladies had worked there faithfully for years, and they must have felt threatened, besides being bored. I did the work of several people, which left little for them to do. Despite all of their strong hints, I had refused to slow down. The foreman knew that with my youthful energy and ambition, I would leave this minimum wage job for a better-paying one as soon as I could (and he was right). He must have concluded that it was wiser to let one worker go now than to later look for four new ones.

OUR SHORT-LIVED HAVEN

Meanwhile, back in Texas, Dad had sweet-talked an elderly neighbor into telling him she had noted California license plates on one of the cars we left in. Dad assumed we had fled to the town of Taft, where Uncle Paul and Aunt Ruth now lived. They were the ones who had taken me to church that eventful night years earlier where I made the choice that changed my life's journey forever.

Dad sent mail to Mom via Uncle Paul, knowing it would be forwarded. At first, Dad tried threats. "If you know what's good for you, you'll get back here with Chuck and Chris. I'm getting tired of this nonsense," his letters warned. When he received no response after sending a number of letters, he changed his tactics. He tried appealing to mother's soft side. "I really need my sweet little wife and children. I miss you so much...I am terribly lonely." Mom continued to ignore his letters.

I found work at the *Turlock Daily Journal*, a few miles away, as a proofreader. Mom, who sewed beautifully, applied for a position as housekeeper and seamstress for a Turlock physician and family. After interviewing her, Dr. and Mrs. Collins introduced her to their children, who liked her immediately. She was hired, but they wanted personal references. Mom gave them the names and addresses of close friends back in Texas whom we trusted. At the top of the list was our pastor's name. "If we can't trust our pastor, who can we trust?" Mom commented as she folded the list and put it into an envelope for her new employer. I agreed. But we were both wrong.

Dad was furious because Mom had gotten away from him despite his threats. He was even angrier because she refused to return. He had lost control of her, and that was unforgivable.

We had no way of knowing it at that time, but Dad really had a heyday at church after we "abandoned" him. Our sudden departure had provided the perfect springboard for his lies.

Dad wept bitter tears before the new pastor, Chad Termilian. (Dr. Hope had retired, and Pastor Termilian had moved into his position.) Dad told everyone at church who would listen about his mistreatment by a deranged wife who had poisoned the minds of his precious children against him—a wife whom he still loved with all of his heart and wanted back despite her wrong actions. Though he had tried to be a perfect father, he said, especially after becoming a Christian, he must have somehow failed God.

Dad was very convincing. After receiving a reference request from Dr. Collins, Pastor Termilian wrote back that mother was so mentally and emotionally incompetent that he could not recommend her for employment. Fortunately, Mom had already established credibility with the Collins family, who found her to be an efficient, responsible, and gentle woman of integrity. They simply did not believe the pastor and gave his letter to Mom. We were shocked, heartbroken, and confused by our former assistant pastor's response.

"Why would Pastor Termilian say something so terrible, Mom?" I cried.

Mother, more angry than tearful, said through clenched teeth, "I suspect Clyde got to him with his conning personality."

"But he knew us just as well as Dr. Hope did. I was president of the Young Women's Auxiliary for a whole year. I was a leader in Sunday school, I sang in the choir, as did you shortly after you joined the church, long before Dad's sudden jailhouse conversion. He knew how Dr. Hope hid us out at the church most of that day when Dad was put in jail. He knew our entire situation." I stood there, shaking my head in puzzlement, tears beginning to spill.

"I know," Mother said sadly and walked away. His stab of betrayal plunged deep into her heart, as it did mine.

We had no way of knowing that Dad was experiencing anything other than anger from a wounded ego of a rejected husband and father who was trying to gain sympathy from the friends of his rebellious wife. Only much later did we realize he was laying the foundation for a diabolical plan. And what better people could he have in his corner than kind and trusting God-fearing people?

❧

Shortly afterwards, we excitedly moved into an inexpensive apartment near downtown Turlock. Granny had already returned to her home in Arkansas. Dad began another barrage of letters, again changing his tactics. "I'm very ill. My ulcers are acting up again, but the doctors aren't sure exactly what's wrong…I'm terribly sick…might even die."

"Good!" Mom said, "I hope he does!"

Determined to obtain a response from Mother, Dad sought yet another direction and aimed straight at the most vulnerable part of her heart: the spiritual spot. Mom, not yet developed in spiritual wisdom and discernment, was quickly impressed by anything that smacked of spirituality. Thus, Dad hit the bull's-eye when after several weeks of silence, he wrote that he had "really gotten religion" and was "really changed."

And yet, who of the wisest and most mature Christians wouldn't be impressed by sentences such as, "I will regret for the rest of my life all the pain I have caused you and the children. I don't blame you for not believing me since I betrayed you with my lies before—when I said I was a new person spiritually but I wasn't. I admit it. I lied because I didn't want to face jail another day. And I'm sorry about the letter from the pastor. I think he just misunderstood some of the things I said, but I'll clear it up. Honey, I really am changed. You see, this is what it has taken for God to get my attention.

"Just think about it, I have no reason to lie now. I've already lost the most precious things on earth to me. I know you and the kids won't come back to me, because you don't believe me. And I don't blame you. I wouldn't believe me, either! I deserve my misery, but you and the kids don't deserve to be miserable—struggling all alone out there—you being so frail and having to work so hard. You deserve better."

Fatigued and weary from overwork and financial struggles, Mom finally succumbed to his persuasion and gave him our address and phone number. When she confessed to me what she'd done, I was terrified!

"Mom! Please don't tell me you did that! How could you?"

Her shoulders sagged. With a deep, pleading sigh she said, "Kitty, he's changed."

"You only think he's changed! I can't believe you fell for his lies! What is it going to take for you to learn?" I lashed out at her angrily, "Now you've endangered all of us—how could you be so stu—" Her crestfallen expression stopped me midsentence, and I couldn't finish.

My anger suddenly evolved into a tight band of protective fear that squeezed my heart so tightly I wanted to scream. I said nothing more. My words held no value now, for they were merely weapons for pain. I reached out and enclosed her delicate, trembling body in my arms and kissed her wet cheeks.

God, help us.

Dad called often. After one long conversation with him, Mom reported that he'd offered to drive to Turlock during his upcoming Christmas vacation and take her and the children back to Texarkana if she'd let him.

"Mom, please don't go back," I begged." I'm not convinced he has changed."

"How can you say that? Where is your faith? Don't you trust God anymore?" she asked, shaking her head in disappointment. As do many of us, Mom had difficulty assessing the fine line between faith and presumption.

"Yes. Of course, I still trust God," I said emphatically. "It's Dad I don't trust."

"You can't see into his heart. You're not God."

"That's true, Mom. But God does give us common sense. He tells us to be cautious in our dealings with others, to be wary." Then I quoted a verse from Jesus's own words: "Look, I am sending you out as sheep among wolves. Be wary as snakes and harmless as doves" (Matthew 10:16).

"But, honey, you read his letters. And you talked to him on the phone just like I did. He apologized to you too. Didn't he say he wanted to spend the rest of his life making it up to me and you kids for all the pain he had caused us? Didn't he say he wanted you to go on to college and not have to worry about anybody but yourself for a change? That's the main reason he said he didn't want you to come back with us—so you could get on with your life." Her eyes pleaded for understanding. "Don't those words evidence a changed heart?"

"I'll admit that Dad's words sound good, Mom," I said with a sigh, "but that's all they are—words. His words alone aren't evidence of anything, other than verbal attempts to get you to do what he wants, which is to go back to him. Remember the last time we trusted his words?"

"But he's never sounded like this before. He's obviously a broken and miserable man."

"I know, Mom," I sympathized, patting her shoulder. "Since we can't see the motive behind a person's words, it is difficult to know when someone is telling the truth. But isn't that all the more reason we need to exercise caution? If we are rushed by words, don't we run the risk of making another wrong choice?"

Despite my strong arguments with Mom, I began to experience my own doubts. *Why should I doubt Dad's spiritual change? I know that there is no one beyond the reach of God's love. No one can do anything so bad that God won't hear an honest prayer from that person and change him. Didn't I myself make a dramatic about-face? Didn't I choose a spiritual course that turned me around completely? While struggling with the idea of shooting my own father, I deliberately made the choice to ask Christ into my life and to help me become the kind of person God created me to be. Why is it so unthinkable that Dad could also make that choice?*

Despite my inner arguments, a knot grew in the pit of my stomach. *I just wish Mom wouldn't rush into this.* But it was no use; her mind was made up. Was it because she actually believed Dad's promises, or was it because she wanted or needed to believe them? I'd heard her crying softly at night, and I marveled at this tiny bundle of strength—a little more than one hundred pounds of it—and the courage she had shown. She constantly battled emotional fatigue and exhaustion, but she tried to present a cheerful attitude for us children. I knew she worried about me and my future. She voiced no hope for my attending college as long as I was burdened with financial responsibilities for my family.

She also worried about Chuck and Chris. They needed a father and a stable home life with adequate food and clothing. Despite his abuse, Dad had always been a hard worker and a good provider. If he were really changed, would she not be morally wrong to stay away from him and subject her children to further deprivation? Sadly, our choices are too often made based upon our wants and our needs rather than upon wisdom.

I too wanted to believe Dad. It would be a relief for me if he *were* changed. Then Mom could take the children back to their home, their roots, and their childhood friends without fear. I could return to work, save my money, and start college the following fall. I could finally pursue my personal dreams.

But deep in my heart, I was bothered by a heavy and familiar sense of foreboding. One that I recognized only too well—one that had always been right.

Despite my pleadings, during her next phone conversation with Dad, Mom agreed to let him drive out and spend Christmas with us. She promised to return to Texas with him, taking Chuck and Chris with them.

THE FATEFUL DECISION

A heavy pall lay over Christmas at our little apartment. The spindly tree, tilting to one side in its stand in the corner, appeared gloomy despite its bright array of ornaments. Dad arrived on December 21, appearing genuinely happy to see us.

Maybe he has changed, I thought. I forced myself to be cheerful, especially for the children, who appeared withdrawn and depressed. Chuck had turned fifteen that fall, and although Dad had promised to buy him a car upon their return, Chuck didn't appear excited.

One day, while Mom and Dad discussed their upcoming trip back to Texas, and Chris sat dejectedly watching TV, Chuck and I quietly cleared the table of its lunch dishes. As I finished putting things away, Chuck walked to the kitchen window. The weather outside was dreary and foggy, matching our general mood. The huge sycamore tree beside the sidewalk near our apartment was bare except for a few stubborn leaves that tenaciously hung on, grasping at life as long as they could.

I observed Chuck from the corner of my eye as he stared forlornly out the window, brows furrowed in deep concentration. *I still think of him as my little brother. When did he grow into a handsome young man?* My heart ached for him. *I wonder if he's thinking about what he almost did that weekend I was gone when he considered shooting Dad following the Fourth of July attack at the park?*

Reflecting back, I pondered the possibility that life had been harder on Chuck in some ways than us girls. He fortunately had more good memories of Dad than Chris and I did. But those few good memories had to have done battle with the overwhelming bad ones. Dad wanted his only son to be a "real man," which, to him, meant Chuck must become proficient in fishing, hunting, and handling a knife, handgun, and rifle. Chuck admitted that while he enjoyed those outdoor trips, he had to be careful. "If I happened to get more squirrels than Dad, I was in danger of getting abused verbally, if not physically."

But even at that, Chuck had quality time with Dad that we girls were denied—because we were girls. I knew this upset Chris, who often expressed to me sadly, "It's not fair. Why can't we go do things with Daddy?" While I certainly didn't want any one-on-one time with Dad, I resented the openly chauvinist favoritism he displayed and the slight that little Chris felt though I was grateful that Chuck at least had some pleasurable experiences with his father. Besides, I knew Chuck needed a healthy outlet for his pent-up emotions, for I rarely saw him cry in our abusive environment. We girls cried easily, and it was a needed release, but Chuck remained stoic. He learned to hide his emotions well—and with good reason. Dad had threatened him ever since he was old enough to understand that "men don't cry, and neither do boys. That makes them sissies. I better not ever catch you crying!" When I considered all things, how could I resent what little joy Chuck got from those rare outdoor excursions?

One weekend, after returning from a hunting trip, Chuck related proudly, "Dad saved my life!" His blue eyes sparkled with excitement. "I was walking in front of Dad through a thicket when suddenly he grabbed me from behind and told me to stand very still. He pointed to the ground. Just in front of me was the biggest coiled rattlesnake I'd ever seen, shaking his rattlers like mad, poised to strike. Dad aimed his rifle and killed that old snake with one shot!" What a wonderful experience for Chuck to finally feel he had value to his father. After all, Dad had saved his life instead of threatening it.

As Chuck stood there, staring out the window but looking at nothing, I wondered if maybe those few good memories didn't dampen his dark plans that near-fatal weekend. Or maybe they were the catalyst that prompted his plans to shoot his father. Could it be that those same sweet memories reminded Chuck of his feelings of bitter betrayal following our father's phony conversion which had lit a strong flame of hope for more pleasant excursions ahead?

I was away that weekend, attending a friend's wedding, and knew nothing of what happened until Chuck told me later.

"I was getting sick and tired of Dad beating up Mom. You know how pretty she is. If some guy looked at her too long or flirted with her when they were out somewhere, Dad would beat her up when they got home. 'I'll teach you to flirt with other men,' he'd snarl. We all know that's why she used to keep her head down most of the time when we were out in public with Dad. And you know how he'd deliberately pick an argument with Mom on Friday evenings just so he'd have an excuse to screech out of the driveway and be gone all weekend."

Oh, yes, I remembered those times.

"This particular Friday evening, Dad started his usual argument. Mom had begun to develop some spunk, and she told him he was cruel. This really set him off. He knocked her down to the floor and started kicking her with his heavy steel-toed boots. She dodged the blows of his boots as best she could, but I could see his kicks were doing serious damage.

"You know how terrified I was of Dad and wouldn't think of confronting him. But watching him viciously kicking Mom that evening really affected me. Maybe it was because you were gone, and I felt the need to be protector, but I suddenly decided I was going to stop all of these beatings and terror once and for all! My usual fear was replaced with a new feeling—a growing desire to see Dad dead.

"After he stormed from the house, I got my .22 rifle out. I recalled how he'd always said, 'Son, never point a gun at anything you don't want to kill.' *Well,* I thought, *this gun is going to be pointed at someone when he walks through that front door, and I mean to kill him—you!*"

I couldn't believe my ears! My little brother was going to shoot our father? My thoughts flashed back to the time I had felt the same way and shuddered. Feeling a wave of guilt, I chastised myself for going away that weekend. *I should have been there protecting my family.*

"Holding my rifle, I plopped down in a chair facing the front door and began my wait. As I sat there, I had flashbacks of a few of the mean things he'd said to me with a sneer. 'If you had any brains in your head as big as marbles, you'd take them out and play with them!' One time when I was younger and I tried to ask him why he was so mean, Dad raised his hand like he was going to hit me. 'If I want anything from you, I'll knock it out of you,' he snarled. Just thinking about that one incident made me want to shoot him even more," Chuck said evenly, his blue eyes growing dark.

"What did Mom say?"

Chuck shrugged. "She didn't take my actions seriously. She looked somewhat surprised though, since I'd never stood up to Dad before. Besides, she was busy nursing her wounds. I could tell she was really in pain as she clutched her side and stomach. Her misery only fueled my resolve to sit there and wait for Dad.

"Saturday morning I awoke in my chair, still clutching the rifle. I laid it down, stretched, and got some oatmeal Mom had fixed and left on the stove. After breakfast and a shower, I was refreshed and so was my resolve. Actually, I was kind of proud of myself for making this stand against Dad. Mom could sense I needed this feeling of being in charge, acting like I was the man of the house, ready to protect my family, so she didn't say anything. She was pretty sure Dad wouldn't return until Sunday evening anyway.

"Saturday night, I again spent the night in the chair facing the front door. I fell asleep, ready to do what needed to be done. Up to this point, had Dad returned, I know I would have shot him.

"Sunday morning, however, when Mom found me asleep still in the chair clutching my rifle, she became worried. She reasoned with me saying how it would ruin my life. Besides, it was a dangerous idea, and why didn't I just go spend such a beautiful day with my buddies doing something fun.

"By this time, my resolve was weakening, and my lifelong fears of Dad returned. I began to visualize Dad grabbing the rifle away from me and beating me to death with it. So I sheepishly put away my rifle and left the house to find my buddies."

With Chuck's confession, I then understood Mom's urgency to get her family away from Dad. It wasn't just because she feared Dad would ultimately kill her and possibly us. She feared what Chuck might do to Dad.

And now, faced with the reality that they would be returning to the lion's den in Texas—with the lion—Chuck had to feel and fear his weighty responsibility of being the sole protector of the lion's prey. And he must wonder if he could rise to the occasion.

Oh, Lord, this burden is too great for my brother. Please give him wisdom and protect them all.

On December 26, as we stood by the loaded trailer, an icy-chilling loneliness crept over me. I gave Dad a perfunctory hug before he went to the car. I turned to little Chris, who clung to me as Chuck shyly waited his turn beside her.

"I don't want to go back. I'm afraid," Chris whispered through quivering lips.

"I know, sweetheart. But Mom needs you to be strong. Just remember, I will be praying for you." I brushed a long blond strand of hair from the side of her face where it was pasted by tears and kissed her good-bye. She turned slowly and trudged toward the car.

Hearing Chris's whisper, Chuck said brusquely, "Me too," as he hugged me long and hard. He wiped at his eyes and quickly turned away. I wanted to be strong for them, but I couldn't keep my tears hidden. They were going back to a terrifying place, and I was staying behind.

Saying good-bye to Mom was the hardest. She wasn't just my mother; she was my dearest and closest friend on earth. A cheery, witty lifter of my spirits—my confidante and my buddy, who often waited up until I returned home from a date to relive the evening with me over hot chocolate and laughter. Hugging her frail body close to me now, I never felt more protective nor more helpless.

"I will miss you so much," she said, between soft sobs. "Please write often."

"You know I'll write, Mom. And I'll be praying for you day and night. I took a deep breath to hold my own emotions at bay. "Don't worry, Mom," I said, mustering a feeble smile. Everything will be okay."

Never did those words sound so empty, nor could they be more untrue.

As I watched the blue and white Ford disappear from sight, my heart twisted with that old feeling of dread. Had this feeling merely become a habit, or was it a genuine premonition of more heartache to come? I shivered and reentered our apartment to finish packing. *Thank God I'll be staying with our pastor and his wife until my tiny apartment is ready*, I thought gratefully. I was already lonely.

LOVE OFFERINGS

As I packed my clothes, I recalled how we had driven the short distance from Uncle John's little town of Delhi to Turlock in search of a church. We believed the words written in the Bible: "And let us not neglect our meeting together, as some people do, but encourage one another" (Hebrews 10:25). God led us to the perfect church, one that opened its loving arms in welcome to our bedraggled and hurting family just as had Uncle John. Shortly after joining that small church, we had moved into this tiny furnished two-bedroom apartment. Scraping up enough money for the usual moving-in costs, we'd had little left over. When the doorbell rang later the same day of our move, we were overwhelmed to see several friends from the church holding large boxes of food. Not only did they contain necessary staples, but also fresh and frozen cartons of meat. Our eyes widened as we took out packages of pork chops, ground beef, wieners, and even steaks—meats that we'd not had for a long time. Every now and then, during the rest of our time there, different church members appeared with more edible love offerings—just at the moment when there was little in our refrigerator and pantry.

Ours was a little church in the midst of a small farming community, and none of its members were wealthy. But it was here that I learned how to give. Oh, I had given canned goods during food drives for the poor in our large church back in Texas. I had felt warm and fuzzy over donating the cans I had carefully selected from our pantry: cranberry sauce left over from the last holiday, beets, sauerkraut, all the off-brand items that I didn't really care about anyway. Stuff we wouldn't miss. But that wasn't giving.

As I resumed packing, I began to understand why God wanted us to become part of a local church family. We needed the love and nurture we received from it—in every way. Though our physical needs were important, our spiritual development needed to experience the laying aside of our fierce pride by accepting from others what they gave in love. As gratitude slowly replaced our pride, our feelings of shame lessened. The church also needed us. It needed an outlet to experience the joy of giving as expressed by Jesus when he said, "When you did it to one of the least of these my brothers and sisters, you were doing it to me!" (Matthew 25:40). *Thank you, God, for leading us to this church and to Pastor*

Whitaker and his family, I prayed. *Without them, I would feel like an orphan right now. And thank you for their son, Don.*

❧

Don and I had started dating shortly after we joined the church. He was tall and handsome, with dark wavy hair and clear blue eyes. I assumed he was in college when he told me he was "in school." I felt uncomfortable when I later learned that he was only sixteen (I was nineteen), but because he was so mature, the age difference didn't prevent us from enjoying each other's company. We dated often, and he became like a member of our family. His sense of humor and unselfish willingness to always help brightened our days. He had his own car, which was a godsend for us when one day we found ourselves suddenly without transportation.

Shortly after I started working at the *Turlock Daily Journal* and Mom was working for the Collins family, we went out one morning to get into our car—but it wasn't where we had parked it. There was no garage or carport with our apartment, so we had to park on the street. "Our car has been stolen!" Mom shouted into the phone minutes later to the police. I listened as she gave the necessary information. Suddenly she paled. "What do you mean it has been repossessed? That car was paid for with cash. Not a penny was owed on it!"

But there was nothing we could do. The car was in Dad's name. We learned later that Dad had taken out a loan against it and deliberately missed the payments so it would be repossessed. Mother had put $2,000 on that car. After a grocery-store worker had dropped a huge commercial-size can of food on her size 4 foot and she had undergone months of painful treatment, she was given $2,000 as a settlement. And I put $500 of my own money in on it, since I knew I would be using it. I complained,

"We are letting him have the house and everything else. How could he do that?"

"We're not 'letting' him have anything, honey. The car is in his name, as is the house and everything back there. We have nothing," Mother said in a matter-of-fact tone.

❧

I slammed some books into a box, anger flaring again. *Lord, I still get mad when I think about that. There we were, barely surviving, and stranded. No money, no car, and no way to get to work. What a dirty trick! And yet I thank you that you helped us find an old car to get to around in.* I lugged the largest suitcase out to the street and opened the trunk of the car. *And thank you, Lord, that Don is so handy with cars and helped us keep this clunker running.* I packed the last of my things into the car and was thankful again for the Whitaker family. Pastor Whitaker and his wife had invited me to stay with them for as long as I needed. It would be temporary, however, as the tiny apartment I had rented would be ready in two weeks. My plan was to continue working at the newspaper and save my money until fall, when I would enroll in college. I knew I'd have to work my way through school, but, with God's help, I was ready to do whatever was necessary.

The tantalizing aroma of pot roast welcomed me as I entered the parsonage carrying my meager belongings. "Ma" Whitaker opened her arms and hugged me as "Pa" grabbed my belongings and whisked them away to my room. I always felt relaxed in this godly home, where I was enveloped by an atmosphere of love so strong that it felt almost tangible. Despite my peaceful surroundings, however, I worried about Mom and the kids and didn't sleep well that first night.

I awoke early the next day exhausted and weary but managed to drag myself to work. Several days later, my mood matched the weather that dreary, foggy early January morning, but I forced myself to concentrate on my job. I had recently been promoted and trained as one of three Linotype operators at the newspaper. One of the operators had injured her wrist over the weekend, so that left the typing of the entire daily newspaper to the other operator and me. It was a hectic day, leaving little time for me to dwell on the growing uneasiness in the pit of my stomach. Shortly after dinner that evening, I excused myself and retired to my room. *I'm glad Don is spending the night with a buddy,* I thought gratefully. *I am so exhausted I don't even have the energy to be sociable.* I dropped into my bed and quickly fell into a deep sleep.

A PREMONITION FULFILLED

In the early morning hours, the jangling of the pastor's phone in his study across the hall from my bedroom jarred the stillness. I forced myself to rise and open my bedroom door slightly. I heard the pastor's voice when he finally answered, but his words were inaudible. I froze with fear, for I knew it was bad news. Perched on the edge of my bed, I shivered and waited.

The pastor rapped softly on my now-open door. Placing his hand on my shoulder, he said gently, "It's your aunt Eunice. She has some bad news." Eunice was my granny's sister, one of our closest relatives living across town from us. My throat suddenly closed. I was barely able to speak into the phone.

"Kitty," Aunt Eunice began gently, "your mom is in the hospital. Your dad tried to kill her, and she is not expected to live."

"Oh, no!" I gasped. "Did he shoot her?"

My great-aunt hesitated, trying to arrange unarrangeable words. "No, honey," she said. "I'm so sorry to have to tell you this…" Fighting for control, she finally sobbed out, "He beat her in the head with a claw hammer while the children were sleeping in the back of the house."

"A claw hammer!" Pain seared my mind as it focused on the mental images burning into it. *The children!* "What about the—"

"Chuck and Chris are safe here with us. We don't know where your dad is. There is an APB out on him, and the police in Turlock have been alerted—we're afraid he might come after you next. I'll call you tomorrow when we learn more."

After I stammered good-bye, my pastor and his wife led me back to my room, where I sobbed out the news. Their faces reflected the horror I felt, but they remained silent until I finished. They gathered me gently into their arms. I felt one with them as their bodies shook with soundless sobs. We knelt and prayed for my mom and for the terrified children. They prayed that my father would be found before further harm was done. They prayed for me, that I would be granted peace, strength, and wisdom to endure this painful moment and the difficult times that lay ahead. I relaxed in the warmth of their love. It comforted me to know that they would continue praying for me through the night. I knew there would be no rest for any of us.

"Please, God, don't let Mom die!" I prayed as I curled into a tight ball in my bed. The next day Aunt Eunice called with an update. "Your dad was arrested and is in the same hospital as your mom. He apparently took an overdose of something and was found semiconscious early this morning in his car parked near the entrance of the waterworks. He was found by an employee on his way to work."

How convenient! I thought. *He's always thinking. Let him die, Lord—he doesn't deserve to live.*

My aunt continued, "Your mother is awake and is calling for you."

Oh, thank You, God. She is still alive!

"The children are okay, but I think they've come down with the measles."

The measles! Lord, you let them come down with the measles?

"Oh, no. Poor things—as if they're not in enough misery already." I asked to speak to them, but they had been quarantined to one room. Aunt Eunice and Uncle Henry lived with their oldest daughter and her husband. "Tell Chuck and Chris that I love them and I miss them. I'll be there as soon as I can."

I collected my paycheck, tied up all the loose ends, and said tearful good-byes to the Whitakers as I prepared to board the train to Los Angeles. Don and I promised to write, but even as we tearfully hugged, I suspected we would never share a future together. We wrote off and on for several months and then gradually stopped as life took us in different directions. During the trip to Los Angeles my train was detained for an hour due to the derailment of another train caused by snow and bad weather. As a result, I missed my connection with the new streamlined Sunset Limited in Los Angeles. I had a three-hour wait in the large cold Union Station.

It was already dark by the time I finally boarded what some of the passengers called the milk train. The train was old, cold, and rickety. I soon discovered it would shuffle to a stop at every tiny town it happened upon. I found an empty row of seats and settled into one.

I slept fitfully during the night, until I was awakened in the early hours of the morning by cold drops of water falling on my head. It was raining and there was a leak above me, so I changed seats. The next morning, I stared gloomily out the window as the rain drenched the gray, barren thirsty desert. Trickles of water ran with force down the outside of the glass. As we passed a large desert bush, I noted a drenched cottontail hunching beneath it for shelter. *Lord, I feel as desolate as that little rabbit. Help us both. But most of all, help Mom. Please let her be alive when I get there.*

ৰ

Aunt Eunice and my cousins met me at the train depot. "Is Mom—" My throat tightened. I couldn't finish the question.

"She's alive, and she's still asking for you." They whisked me quickly to the hospital. When I entered Mom's room, I saw

Granny sitting by Mom's bedside, where she had been day and night since her arrival. She arose quickly and hugged me long and hard.

"Thank You, God, for bringing Kitty here safely," she whispered. I clung to her and kissed her soft, wrinkled face, wet with tears of joy at my arrival.

Granny had always cried easily. We used to tease her about her free-flowing tears. Always when we arrived at our step-grandfather McAllister's farm, Granny would descend upon us, mouth quivering and tears flowing. "Why are you crying, Granny?" we'd say through the rolled-down car windows. "Aren't you happy to see us?" We'd laughingly ask, knowing the answer.

"Yes, I'm happy to see you, but I don't want you to leave."

Tumbling out of the car, we would hug her and say, "Granny, we're not leaving. We're arriving."

"I know," she'd respond sheepishly. "But you're going to be leaving in a week."

I turned toward Mom's bed. I don't know what I expected, but I wasn't prepared for what I saw. Swathed in bandages from the neck up, her head swollen to twice its normal size, Mom looked like a gigantic mummy from a horror movie. There were only slits for her eyes, nose, and mouth.

"Oh, Mom," I cried, rushing to her. Though it was difficult for her to speak, little by little she filled me in on what happened that fateful night.

After the children went to bed, Mom said she had developed a sudden severe headache. Dad gave her a pill for her discomfort that we later learned was a barbiturate of some kind called a "yellow jacket"—something to knock her out completely. He had wanted no interruptions while he carried out the diabolical plan he had formed before he went to California and brought her back. Once she was asleep, Dad took a claw hammer and methodically beat her in the head and temples until he thought she was dead. He then quietly left the house and drove away.

In the early morning hours, Mom regained consciousness. Her eyes were swollen shut, and she couldn't see. She wondered why she felt wet and sticky over her entire body. She knew it wasn't sweat—it was too thick. Besides, it was winter.

Something is terribly wrong, she thought. She believed that whatever it was, my dad was responsible. The house was deathly quiet, but she wasn't sure he was gone. Worried about the children, she slowly groped her way down the hall to Chris's room, the nearest to her. Nudging Chris awake, she whispered in the darkness. "Go wake your brother. We've got to leave. And don't turn on the light."

"But what—?"

"Shhh. I don't know where your dad is, but something is wrong. Go get Chuck. We've got to get to the hospital."

"The hospital?"

"Just go get him, honey. Hurry!"

Chris returned shortly with a groggy Chuck stumbling behind her. Mom felt for and found their hands, and the three of them padded softly into the living room. When the harsh yellow of the outside streetlight fell across Mom through the window, Chris started screaming. To her, Mom appeared as a crimson, slimy monster. She was bloody from head to foot. Her blood-soaked gown clung to her thin body. Puffed eyelids protruded from her face, already swollen shut beyond recognition. Mother, fearing for their lives, shushed her to be quiet. She asked Chuck to dial the operator for her, and she asked that an ambulance be sent. Minutes later the ambulance came and transported them to the hospital.

"You know the rest of the story, honey," Mom said weakly. I squeezed her hand and insisted she rest. I feared she had overdone it. *I shouldn't have let her talk so much,* I chided myself.

"We'll talk more tomorrow, but for now you need your rest, Mom." My throat tightened, and I felt I couldn't breathe as I considered all she had told me. "I love you so much, Mom. I can't imagine life without you. You will come through this. God will help you, and so will the rest of us."

Suddenly, I felt exhausted. I slid into an empty chair near Granny close enough to Mom's bed to still hold her hand. Granny arose and tucked the covers in around Mom. We sat there in silence until we heard Mother's even breathing.

Speaking softly so as not to disturb Mom, Granny related her amazing story of how God spoke to her that same tragic night.

"I was sound asleep," Granny said, "when I heard my name called. 'Mary, wake up.' I stirred a little, but I was so tired and sleepy I just couldn't seem to move. Again, the voice said, more commanding, 'Mary, wake up!' This time I awoke and sat straight up in bed, looking around in the darkness. The voice said, 'Esther needs you. Get up and pack your suitcase, and be ready.'"

She and Grandpa McAllister lived about one hundred miles north of us on their farm out in the country. They had no phone service, and their closest neighbor with a phone was Grandpa's son Cecil who lived about a mile away. Granny said she got up, explained to Grandpa what was happening, packed a suitcase, and moved it into the hall, where she sat down to wait. She didn't know for who or what.

A short time later, she saw car lights turning onto the road to their house. Someone bounded up the steps onto the front porch and banged loudly on the door. Granny opened it, and Cecil said breathlessly, "Esther is bad hurt in a Texarkana hospital. I need to take you to the bus terminal."

Granny said she smiled feebly as he looked surprised at her suitcase. "Yes, I know," she said, "and I'm ready." They got to the bus station just in time for her to catch the bus before it pulled out—the last bus going to Texarkana until the next day.

"The following day," Granny said, "I got a phonebook and began calling pastors of different churches all around Texarkana. A number of them came to your mom's hospital room, formed a prayer circle around her bed, and we all prayed that her life would be spared."

I thanked God for my devout God-loving Granny. I gave her a big hug and, choking back a sob, said, "I can't imagine how terrible it would be if you weren't here. For all of us. And thanks to God's message, you got here when you did." We slept in our chairs that night near my mom, each of us continuing our prayer vigil.

As Mom continued to hover between life and death, the doctors sadly explained to Granny and me that it was unlikely she would survive. They were trying to prepare us for what they believed was the inevitable, but we both kept praying for a miracle.

Thus, it was that I again became a supporting member of my hurting family.

THE PAINFUL PATH

I don't know why, but I kept thinking of Dad lying in his hospital bed on the floor just above us. Like the tongue is drawn irresistibly to the empty socket of a missing tooth, my mind returned to the idea of sneaking up and taking a peek into Dad's room. I didn't want to talk with him, nor did I want him to see me, but for some strange reason, I wanted to go to his room and observe him unnoticed. The idea wouldn't go away.

My second day there, I took the elevator up to Dad's floor and located his room. The chair next to the wall just outside his room was empty. *The guard must be taking a break,* I thought gratefully. I didn't want anyone to know I was there. *If Dad's awake,* I decided, *I'll just step back and not enter. Lord, please let him be asleep.* I peeked through the partially open door. Dad's head rested on a pillow, his face turned slightly toward the opposite wall. Holding my breath, I inched the door open a little wider. I was relieved when I saw his mouth open in deep sleep. He was unshaven, and his wavy brown hair, which he took such pride in, was tousled and looked dirty. Both wrists were chained to the metal frame of his bed.

He's chained there like a wild, helpless, dirty animal! I thought. Sudden pity flooded my heart. *How sad!* But the feeling lasted only for a moment. My emotions then ran rampant.

Feelings of anger and hate wrestled with pity and disgust deep within me. Good memories and bad memories jostled in a mind that didn't know what to think. Past scenes of my childhood played across the screen of my mind—times when I crawled into Dad's lap, plying him with hugs and kisses, trying to draw from him something that would fill the emptiness of my childish heart for at least a moment. *I will be so good and loving that he will stop being bad and then he will love me!* My childish mind had vowed. But my love wasn't strong enough to change him into a good father.

I recalled how, despite my fear and hate for him at times, as I grew older, my hungry heart pushed me to try and elicit affection from him verbally. "Do you love me, Daddy?"

Most often he responded irritably with, "What do you think? I go to work every day to provide you with food, clothing, and a place to live. Doesn't that show you that I love you?"

No, it didn't. That wasn't enough. As I grew older, I recalled thinking, *Would he stop working and doing all those things if he didn't love me? And what about the way he treats us? If he really loved us, why was he so mean?* Ultimately, I gave in to frustration and decided, *I don't know why I even care!*

There had been happy times when Dad made us laugh, when he was demonstrative, but they were overshadowed by our fear. We could only enjoy those moments guardedly. We realized they would soon be buried beneath more layers of hurt, distrust, and fear, for we knew the good moments wouldn't last.

I don't know how long I stood there gazing at the man who was not only my father but also my enemy. *How can this be, Lord? I don't know what to feel. Do I hate him or do I pity him? My heart is numb. I feel like I should pray right now—but I don't know what to say. Please help me.* I tiptoed to the door and peered out. The guard's chair was still empty.

Several days later Dad was discharged and taken to jail.

THE SCENE OF THE SHADOW OF DEATH

One of my most difficult duties was to return to our home. A friend drove me there and, at my insistence, continued on to do her grocery shopping. For some strange reason, I wanted to be alone. Was it because I was ashamed for anyone else to see evidence of that night's horror? Or was this just another in succession of a lifelong line of duties that I alone felt responsible for carrying out?

Accompanied only by the tall leafless oak trees, twisted, ugly, and grotesque in their nakedness as they loomed over me in the front yard, I stood on the front walk and waited. For what? *Am I ready to face what I will see inside?* I shivered as I fumbled with the key in the lock, dreading the moment of entry.

The living room looked much the same, except for some clutter. Newspapers lay scattered on the coffee table and floor. But it was eerie as I entered the dining room. A huge pot of Mother's delicious homemade stew, now caked and hard, sat in the middle of the table. Dishes with crusty, partially eaten food were still in their places. Dirty glasses, some with curdled, dry milk, stood by their plates. It was as though everyone were suddenly whisked away.

The rest of the rooms were chaotic, with drawers open, some partially empty on the floor, and their contents strewn about. Disarray was everywhere—exactly as the investigative officers had left things in their search for clues behind this horrendous crime. Clues had been found in letters that Dad had written to someone, we never learned who, which described his plan to murder Mom. This evidence led to his charge of premeditated attempted murder.

The last room—and the hardest for me to enter—was the scene of the crime, my mom and dad's bedroom. I stood before the closed door, trembling, suddenly afraid to touch the knob. Was I really prepared for what was on the other side? Could I handle it even with God's help? I wasn't sure. I took a deep breath, slowly turned the knob, and gently pushed open the door.

The bed and all its gore loomed in full view. The rumpled sheets and pillows were a tangled mass of stiff, bloodied fabric. The sheer white curtain panels on the window near the bed, mute witnesses to the room's horror, bore a macabre pattern of random dark blotches running from their top ruffle down to the floor.

Magenta marks tracked back and forth across the floral patterned carpet. Crimson stains, stark against the pale white embossed wallpaper, streaked upward onto the ceiling. With wide, unblinking eyes, I followed the path of the stain's ultimate destination onto the vaulted ceiling. I caught my breath as the viciousness of the attack penetrated my dumfounded mind. *These walls are ten feet high!*

The bedspread, blankets, and quilts were folded back at the end of the bed and showed only minimal evidence of what took place. It struck me as strange that such care would be taken to spare bedclothes the same carnage that was planned for the bed's inhabitant, my mom. I fell against the wall, sobbing.

Lord, I don't know if I can do this. Please give me strength to clean all of this up, I prayed. I knew Chuck would have helped me, but though he was a teenager, I still thought of him and protected him as a child—my child. And hadn't he been through enough already? He was here in this house, as was Chris, that terrible night! As I leaned against the wall, trying to compose myself, I recalled his recollection of what happened.

"I was sound asleep that night in my back bedroom, dreaming of the wonderful car Dad had promised me if we came back. In reality, it was only an old black Ford Coupe (1940s vintage) and I didn't have a driver's license yet, but at least I'd have my very own car. I was so excited in my dream—my life was finally making a turn for the better.

"I was wrestled out of my happy dream by someone persistently calling my name in a loud whisper. I fought to stay asleep, but the voice became urgent, and louder, 'Chuck, wake up. Mom needs you.' It was Chris tugging on my arm.

"I swung out of bed and stumbled into our living room behind her. I was shocked wide awake by the scene before me. Mom was standing there swaying, blood covering her face, neck, and nightgown, and dripping on the carpet. I could see white bones protruding through the gaping bloody wounds on both sides of her face. My heart froze with horror. Mom said calmly, 'Charles, I need you to dial the operator for me—I can't see.'

"I was terrified! Where was Dad? I knew he had done this. Would he come lunging into the room any second and finish the job he'd started and kill Chris and me too? I grabbed the phone and dialed the operator. Still calm, Mom said, 'Now put it in my hand.' She then spoke into the phone clearly and distinctly, 'Operator, would you please send me an ambulance, I think I'm dying.'

"After she gave the operator our address, she handed me the phone, but my hands were shaking so badly I could barely place it back into its cradle. Chris, who had started screaming and backing away when she first saw Mom in the light from the streetlight shining through our window, was now sobbing quietly and shaking violently as she moved closer to me. I guided Mom to a chair, where she sat until the ambulance arrived only minutes later. That wait seemed like an eternity.

"Hearing the siren on our street, I quickly opened the door, and two medics rushed inside. They stopped suddenly, mouths dropping open, when they saw Mom. They thought she had been shot on one side of the head with the bullet coming out the other side of her face and marveled that she was even alive. They quickly strapped Mom on a gurney and put her, Chris, and me in the back of the ambulance."

Recalling Chuck's narrative, presented with such clarity, I could almost feel the pain he experienced in retelling it. Suddenly, it was difficult for me to breathe. I realized I had been holding my breath, despite my heart's furious pounding, as I relived my brother's tale of horror. I took a slow deep breath before recalling the rest of his painful story.

"I was so frightened but couldn't show it. I knew Chris was horrified, and I had to be strong for her. She trembled beside me in the ambulance, but her sobs slowly subsided into silent terror. We didn't know if Mom would live long enough to get to the hospital. Once we arrived, I felt a little better and whispered to Chris, 'We're here now, and Mom will get help. Everything is going to be okay." But as the two attendants were taking Mom out of the ambulance, a nurse rushed outside yelling, 'You can't bring anyone here! We're all filled up with patients. There's no room!'"

"My heart sank. Chris started crying again, and I felt like it, but I forced every ounce of my strength to hold back my tears. I silently prayed for Mom as they quickly loaded her back into the ambulance. With sirens again screaming, we headed for the only other hospital miles across town. By that time I was shaking with terror. I moved forward slightly so Chris couldn't feel my tremors, pretending to look out the window toward the front. I had entered first after Mom was strapped in so I could help Chris up. For Chris's sake, I kept my tears at bay, but inside I was weeping. *Poor Mom, how can she possibly survive? Please, God, you must help her.*

"The next thing I remember, Chris and I were sitting just outside the emergency room waiting as they began to work on Mom. I started to relax a little, knowing Mom would finally receive the help she so desperately needed. But my hope suddenly dissolved into stunned disbelief when I heard the doctor yell to the nurse, 'Just clean this woman up and put her in a room—she's too far gone. She's dying. We can't help her!' So they cleaned her head and bandaged it. No blood transfusion, no surgery, just bandages. They then stuck her in a room to die. Chris and I were frozen with fear. How could we live without our loving mother? And what would happen to us if she died?"

I forced myself back to the present. *No, I will clean all of this alone. It's the least I can do since they've been through so much already. They would be devastated if they saw this! But as I perform this heartbreaking task, Lord, please don't let me be consumed with hate for my father.*

It took several trips to do what had to be done and to put everything back into place. Each trip was an exercise in faith, determination, and prayer. Finally, with a power that came only from God, everything was ready for our return.

Our first night home was difficult. I asked Chris to sleep with me until she felt secure enough to sleep alone. I feared that her recurring nightmares of that terrible night and her ride in the ambulance might worsen.

Chris had been terrified. When Mom suddenly became motionless and stopped moaning in pain, she thought our mother had died. She watched in silent terror as mother's still form swayed eerily with every motion of the ambulance, her blood spilling onto the floor. With each turn, the end of the gurney swayed into Chris and jostled her. The fear that her mother's blood might drip onto her and her nightclothes intensified Chris's terror. *Chris will need to sleep with me a long time,* I decided.

And deep inside, I knew I needed her company too.

I prayed for continued strength and wisdom as I dealt with our everyday problems. Besides spending most of each day with Mom at the hospital, I filled out medical insurance forms and dealt with living expenses. Our house was paid for, but we had no income. The savings account had been cleaned out, and there was no checking account. All we had to live on was the money I had brought with me and a little Granny had forced me to take. She and Grandpa McAllister had very little, and they struggled to survive on their rocky-soiled farm. Fortunately, the owner of the newspaper in Turlock had given me some extra money out of his pocket when I left, as had the Whitakers. *I have to find a job soon,* I worried, *but that's not going to be easy.* The family car had been impounded for evidence when Dad was arrested, and I had no transportation. With the kind help of many wonderful friends, neighbors, and a good bus system, I was able to get around. Soon I found work and brought in enough money for us to survive.

One morning, as I stood at the bus stop in freezing rain, I saw our family car go by with someone whom I didn't recognize at the wheel. After arriving at work, I called the sheriff's department and was told it was still impounded. When I explained that I had just seen it, they said I was mistaken. We later learned that it had been sold—to someone in the sheriff's department. I had forgotten that the car was still in my father's name. Dad had used the money from its sale to hire a private attorney. He didn't want to use the one appointed by the court. (Following the trial, Dad's attorney forced us to give him $300 for the deed to our house, which Dad had given him, even though the court had awarded the house to us.)

After twenty-six long, painful days, Mom was discharged from the hospital. One of the doctors admitted, "We had little to do with her survival—it was obviously the work of God." We rejoiced upon her discharge, but shortly after arriving home, she developed lockjaw. For weeks, the only nutrition she received was through a straw. She ultimately overcame that discomfort, but her private pain—physical and mental—would continue for a lifetime. Dad's stay in the hospital had been very brief. We were convinced that his "overdose" had been merely a sympathy-getting ploy to lay groundwork for his temporary insanity plea, which we were certain he would use. Shortly after he was transported to jail, he was released on bail with instructions not to leave the state. His freedom, however, made us again his prisoners.

We nailed our windows shut and put deadbolts on our doors. Despite these precautions, we were still afraid to go to sleep at night. With no air conditioning and only small fans to rearrange the hot air, the humid Texas nights were almost unbearable.

I found a better-paying job as a night proofreader at the *Texarkana Gazette* and began dating Floyd Moore, a co-worker who had graduated from my high school the same year as I. Floyd was a special angel sent by God to befriend me and my bedraggled family during this dark time. He had friends on the police force who were kind and concerned enough to patrol the front and back of our house day and night, on and off duty. We were comforted by the lights from the patrol cars as they crept in slow motion down the alley behind our house at night, making it easier for us to sleep.

᱐

Each time we made the trip to the courthouse, emotionally prepared for the ordeal of Dad's trial, we left disappointed and angry. Dad's attorney always appeared without our father, stating that Dad was "sick." It seemed this frustrating chapter in our lives would never end.

In reality, Dad was never sick. He was out of state. We children began receiving letters from him postmarked in California. Though he never wrote Mother, we knew these letters were written for her benefit. They were sickeningly sweet, telling us how much he loved and missed us. One letter included photos of him at the beach with three scantily clad attractive young women clinging to him.

"Aren't my girlfriends cute?" his handwriting taunted from the back of one photo. One letter addressed to me contained three ten-dollar bills—the only money we ever received from him. He said it was for us children to spend on something "fun" for ourselves. When I showed Mom the letter, she crumpled the bills, threw them on the floor, and stomped on them. She then calmly picked them up, smoothed them out, and we used them for groceries.

Several weeks later, we learned that Dad had returned from California. There were rumors that he was going out of his way to be friendly, looking up old family friends, shaking hands with everyone he had known, seen, or met as though he were on a political campaign trail. He encountered Granny one day at the bus station, just as she arrived in town, where he loudly begged her forgiveness for his "one mistake" to her daughter. When he extended his hand, Granny snarled, "Do you really think I would shake your hand! Get away from me." We never learned how he knew she was arriving by bus to visit us that day. That only made us more frightened to realize he knew so much about what was happening in our lives. It made us suspicious of friends, of whom one must be an "informant."

Finally, five months following Mom's discharge from the hospital, Dad appeared in court for his trial. We weren't surprised at Dad's temporary insanity plea, but we were surprised by the method he used to attempt to try to substantiate it. Neither were we prepared for the humiliation it would bring.

The defense stated that my mother and I were prostitutes in our home. Dad was depicted as a devoted family man who came home early one night and caught his wife in bed with another man. That was shocking enough, they said, but when he learned that his beautiful daughter was also a prostitute, he was devastated and blamed his wife for her bad example. (Strangely, that was the first time I ever heard my father describe me as beautiful. I grew up hearing him call me ugly and stupid.) The defense explained that when the defendant stumbled upon the dirty truth, he simply couldn't handle it. He became so distraught that he committed this crime—for which he was now "deeply sorry."

After the defense set the perfect stage for his entrance, Dad gave a flawless performance on the stand—even to the point where he broke into sobs after uttering the sad words, "And that's how I found out about the immoral activities of my sweet wife and precious daughter."

We were torn by the injustice of the situation. It seemed that we, the victims, were now on trial as everyone in the packed courtroom turned and glared at us. A parade of character witnesses for my dad flocked to the stand and declared his goodness under oath, stating that he was "incapable of hurting even a fly."

Though their testimony pained me, I realized these were sincere people who really believed what they were saying. Many of them had known or worked closely with my father for ten years. But they had no way of knowing what he was really like. They saw only what my father wanted them to see. Besides, who wouldn't believe such a kind-appearing man, head in hands, sobbing, obviously heartbroken over the tragic turn of events in his life?

When the reality of the defense's statement penetrated my mind, a feeling of hot shame suddenly poured over me. As a young woman who had never "known a man" in the biblical sense, such an accusation was unbearable. And how my heart ached for my mother. *Poor little Mom! This is adding insult to injury! How can they lie like this in court and get away with it?*

Everything that followed appeared in silent slow motion. I saw my tiny granny rise to her feet and cry out, "That is a filthy lie!" but my numb mind heard nothing. I saw the judge pound his gavel and call out "order in the court," but I heard no sound. I watched my granny's lips move again and the judge threaten to have her removed from the courtroom if there were further outbursts. I was suspended, frozen within a sphere of soundless, silent pain, one that would haunt me for years.

The people subpoenaed in our behalf, friends who were to declare to the world our good character, never appeared. The pastor of our church, who had given Mom a bad reference while we were in Turlock, had left the area before our return, so I again attended the same church, where I was loved and supported by some of my close friends there. But it hurt that not one of them or any of our other friends appeared in court to support us. We learned later that they didn't want to "be involved."

Even more painful were the remarks later made by an acquaintance, who said, "Well, where there's smoke there's bound to be fire. Why would your own father lie about something like that?" Someone else commented, "Well, your mom must have enjoyed being knocked around, otherwise, she wouldn't have stayed with him all those years."

Though I was deeply hurt, I understood. How could I expect outsiders to look beyond the persuasive powers of my charismatic father? And how could I expect ignorant people, who knew nothing about the helpless feelings of battered women, to understand?

After five hours of deliberation, the jury finally convicted my father of premeditated attempted murder and sentenced him to three and a half years in prison. Since the maximum sentence for premeditated attempted murder at that time in Texas was fifteen years, we felt humiliation rather than vindication. It was apparent that the jury believed Dad was guilty—there was too much evidence substantiating his crime, including his tearful admission of guilt—but some of them obviously also believed what was said about Mom and me. Out of sympathy for the defendant, they had given him the minimum sentence.

Though we stung from that light sentence, we were thankful that Dad had been convicted, even for a short time. At last we were free.

DON'T ASK ME TO FORGIVE!

Following Dad's trial, he threatened to "get us" upon his release. He blamed us for his conviction and vowed to make us pay someday. But we were free now—at least for three-and-a-half years, maybe less, depending upon the parole board.

We would later learn that he was released six months early due to good behavior. Would he find us after his release? Would we have to keep running?

We pushed his threats to the back of our mind as we put our house up for sale and made our plans to move to California. Mom and I excitedly looked up information about the Golden State. We didn't want to move too close to relatives because we didn't want to be a burden, yet we wanted to live close enough to visit them from time to time. We loved the ocean, but we also loved the mountains. We wanted to live in a city that wasn't too large, yet was big enough to provide employment opportunities. Where could we find such a perfect place?

Despite our newfound freedom from fear, I wasn't happy. Fear had disappeared, but anger spread quickly to fill its place. I was growing angrier each day.

One morning, as I was sorting through the things I would either take or get rid of, I recalled the first time we had fled to California and how frustrated I was at having to decide what to take or leave behind. I recalled how I, as the oldest child, had assumed an unrealistic responsibility for my siblings and mother when I was very young—a burden far too heavy for the small shoulders of a child. *And it still seems too heavy,* I thought, my anger flaring.

Dad has caused me a lot of pain! I thought, tossing some items into the "for rummage" box. *Not only did he force adult burdens on me, he robbed me of the love and security every child should experience. Instead, I lived in constant fear—in the past and even now. Fear that he would find us and fear of what would happen when he did find us. Will I always have to live in fear?* Not even the loving arms of the man I married two years later could protect me from recurring nightmares of Dad chasing me with a gun.

I was also angry because of the shame I felt that day in the courtroom when Mom and I had been called prostitutes in front of strangers. It would be years before I could watch a trial on television or in a movie without leaving the room in tears.

Though I loved the Lord and had continued to worship him at the church where we were all baptized, bitter weeds of resentment sprang up rapidly in the fertile soil of my anger. *My father has caused every pain in my life, and he is still causing me problems. It's not fair,* I decided, kicking an empty box into the corner. I didn't realize it then, but the anger I harbored was destructive. If I continued this line of thinking, my thoughts would develop patterns that would spread tenacious roots into every nook and cranny of my mind. If left unchecked and allowed to grow, they would produce fruit of their own kind, tempting fruit that, once tasted, could lure me into a vicious mental cycle. For, oh, how sweet are those first few bites of the victim mentality.

With the mind-set of a victim, even if I never saw my father again, I could blame him for all of life's difficulties. I could develop the habit of blaming others for my problems and thus avoid responsibility for my own actions. I could eventually even blame God for dealing me such a bad hand. After all, why should I be held accountable for anything in life? I was born a victim and I would always be a victim.

But God had different plans. Once again, he sent someone to help me. Not long after Dad was sent to prison, an older woman at church asked me, "Have you forgiven your father?"

I was shocked. *Forgive my father! My emotional wounds are still raw and bleeding; how dare she speak to me about forgiveness!*

"My father will never ask me to forgive him for anything—so I don't think I'll have to worry about it," I said crisply.

Her eyes were gentle and her voice soft as she said, "You may be right—but you still need to forgive him."

"Why should I do that?" I snapped. "He doesn't deserve forgiveness."

"Again, you are right, but you still need to forgive him."

"I'd like to know just who, in his right mind"—*since I'm sure you aren't in yours*—"would expect me to forgive my father after all he has done to us!"

She was quiet for a long moment. Finally she answered, "God."

I said nothing more, but inwardly I seethed. *Had she gone through what my family had, she wouldn't be standing there in her unscarred composure blithely advising me to forgive!* The scars on my mother's temples were still swollen, red, and angry—just like the anger swelling within me. *And I was supposed to think about forgiveness?*

I was irritated, but I wasn't going to let her unrealistic statements about forgiveness dampen my enthusiasm for our upcoming family move.

We were excited! Our spunky mother obtained her driver's license, and after the sale of our house, we bought an inexpensive new car, a 1955 blue and white Fairlane Ford, and a used trailer to haul what household items we would take with us. Soon we would be heading west to the beautiful state of California, which had everything: mild climate, azure-blue ocean, warm sand, green valleys, the beautiful Sierra mountains, crystal clear streams, lots of job opportunities, and a new beginning. Not to mention Disneyland, Yosemite, and Fisherman's Wharf!

But the woman's comments about forgiveness sharpened the teeth of conviction that continued to nip at me. I knew I needed to forgive Dad, but I wasn't ready to let go of my resentment.

Not yet. *Soon we'll be gone, and I won't be reminded of her comments because I'll never see her again,* I consoled myself. So I pushed it to the back of my mind.

Despite my resolve to not think about the forgiveness issue, from time to time, it popped into my mind. And I argued. *My father doesn't deserve my forgiveness. What he really deserves is something worse than what he got! Only three-and-a-half years for premeditated attempted murder! If anyone has a right to hate and resent, it's my family and me.*

GOD NEVER GIVES UP

But I had a problem. I knew that the Bible had much to say about forgiveness. Though I read my Bible diligently, I picked and chose the truths I wanted to relate to and ignored the ones I didn't want to deal with. I loved reading about the "goodies" in the Bible—how much God loves me, how he would never leave me nor forsake me, and how nothing on earth could separate me from his love. Those were great verses!

I rejoiced over the verses that talked about how all the "bad" guys were going to "get it," how they would one day stand before God, be found guilty, and then finally pay for their wrongdoings. The only problem with those verses was that I didn't want to wait until some future day of judgment. I wanted to see them get what was due them *now.* Besides, why should I concern myself about forgiving someone who had not yet even begun to pay for his wrongs?

I knew, however, that this special relationship between my heavenly Father and me was never meant to be one-sided. The Bible made it clear that Christ was not only my Savior and friend, he was also my Lord. As my friend, I knew he would encourage and comfort me through all the rough spots in life. I also knew a real friend would never lie to me. Christ would always guide me toward honesty and truth, even when I tried to hide behind a wall of denial.

I didn't need great spiritual wisdom to understand that God is not someone to call just to help me out of jams. God was not created for me; I was created for him. And once I accepted him as Lord of my life, he expected me to trust his wisdom and obey him in every area of life, even when I didn't understand. This included forgiving others, specifically my father.

Deep in my heart, I wanted to live up to God's expectations of me by doing my part. The problem was I wanted to choose which parts—the easy parts. So I focused mostly on the "thou shalt nots." Not bow down to any false gods? Why would I do that? I had a relationship with the living God!

Not take God's name in vain? Remember the Sabbath, and honor my father and mother? No problem there. I'd never developed the habit of swearing, I enjoyed going to church, and I loved and respected my mother. I didn't respect my father, of course, but with God's help, I had treated him with respect.

Not kill anyone? Well, when I accepted Christ into my life, that desire went away. After all, I had never really *wanted* to kill my father; I just wanted him to stop hurting us.

Not commit fornication or adultery? Of course, I had been tempted in that area, but my mind was made up. I definitely was going to remain sexually chaste until my wedding day. After all, it was my choice.

Not steal from my neighbor? Piece of cake. I didn't have a problem in that area even before I was a Christian (not unless you count stealing flowers from the neighbor's yard).

Not covet what my neighbors had? No problem there. I may have wanted some things just like what they had, but I never wanted theirs.

Yes, my score seemed pretty good in the Old Testament "thou shalt not" category!

But what about the New Testament commandment summarization by Jesus when he said, "You must love the Lord your God with all your heart, all your soul, and all your mind" and "Love your neighbor as yourself" (Matthew 22:37, 39)? It was a lot easier to not do the things I wasn't supposed to do than to do the things I was *supposed* to do.

God had a way of nudging my thoughts to the "thou shalt" scriptures—the verses that tell us to forgive those who wrong us, to love our enemies and pray for them, to bless those who persecute us, and to be accountable for our own actions, which included even our thoughts. Those were the tough ones!

The closest I ever wanted to get to praying for those who wronged me was similar to that of an old Yiddish prayer I once heard. In this prayer a man prayed, "God, bless the man I hate with a million dollars—and may he give it all to the doctors."

Choosing my thoughts, much less controlling them, seemed impossible. I equated thoughts with feelings, which somehow just happened and you couldn't help them. As my thoughts continued to wrestle with the subject of forgiveness, however, I realized I again had to make a choice.

Two paths stretched before me. I could choose the path of resentment and remain an embittered prisoner, or I could choose the path of forgiveness and be set free. But the path of forgiveness, when compared with the fiery road of resentment, definitely felt less appealing. How I resented having to leave my hometown and all that was dear to me a second time because of my father's threat to harm us following his release! Wasn't robbing me of a normal and happy childhood enough? Tears burned the underside of my lids. *And now he's robbing me of my future because I can't go to college!*

I loved my mom and siblings and would never abandon them, but the unfairness of my situation drove me to constantly blame the only one who *was* responsible for altering my future—my father. *I shouldn't be the one supporting our family, it should be Dad!*

That's his job! Recalling every wrong committed by my father fanned bitter embers of resentment into roaring flames. And yet, the steady beckoning light of my Lord's beaming love continued to distract my dark thoughts. Like a beacon, this love drew my vision toward the only path leading out of darkness to freedom—forgiveness. But how could I find the strength to forgive my father when everything within me screamed for vengeance?

Following my spiritual commitment six years earlier, I had formed the habit of consistently searching the Scriptures for anything that could help me survive my circumstances. Though I hadn't always understood their wisdom nor always lived up to them, I had often proved their power as I applied their principles. Recalling the many times I had been able to do what the Scriptures encouraged me to do gave me hope that maybe I could also someday forgive my father.

Would God be a just God, I thought, *if he commanded me to do something that he knew was impossible for me to do—and then hold me accountable for not doing it? Surely not.* As I struggled with these thoughts one day, I recalled a remarkable event from my past. Something short of a miracle.

When I think of it, from a human standpoint, it seems impossible that a person could face death at gunpoint and not be overcome by fear. And yet, hadn't I been able to do that very thing the night Dad held his gun to my head and threatened to pull the trigger? God had given me faith that prevented fear at one of the most dramatic moments of my life. Could he not also give me the power to forgive? The answer had to be an unequivocal *yes!*

Well, then why hadn't he?

I didn't realize it then, but I was waiting for God to do something that he wasn't going to do. And God was waiting for me to do what only I could do. So we were at a stalemate. But God is patient. He has plenty of time.

CALIFORNIA OR BUST

Our spirits were high as we arrived at our California destination—Santa Barbara—a haven nestled between the rugged coastal mountains and the sparkling sea. As we drove down Highway 101, the early morning sun danced across the blue Pacific Ocean and highlighted the beach that beckoned to us with all its beauty.

Mom and I found work immediately—Mom as a nurse's aide at Cottage Hospital and I as a proofreader for the Santa Barbara News Press. Chuck and Chris were enrolled in school, and we began our new life. For the first six months, we lived in Bam's Auto Court. It was cramped for the eight of us—Mom, me, Chuck, Chris, Fluffy, our white cat, and two canaries—but we were happy.

Our first week there, I located a church and became involved, but Mom refused to go. She had been so hurt by our Texas pastor's betrayal that she couldn't trust Christians. And I couldn't blame her. Though I attended church, I had my own problems. I didn't trust Christians either.

The rip that had started in the lining of my heart with our Texas pastor's betrayal widened when none of our Christian friends appeared in court to support us at the trial. The tear extended so deep and hurt so bad that I had made a vow: *I will go to church and serve the Lord because I love him, but I will never let anyone get close to me again.*

I didn't blame God because of man's failures. Just as Dad's bad choices were not my fault, neither was it God's fault when his family members made wrong choices. I let a scab form over my heart—a scab of protection—as I again became involved in the church.

So I understood when Mother lashed out at me angrily as I wrote out my small tithe check each payday. "You're taking food right out of our mouths when you give money to those people down at that church! How can you be so callous?"

I knew she didn't understand, that I wasn't giving money to "people" or "that church"—I was only giving back to God what was due him. But it still hurt, for I loved my mother dearly. Though our financial circumstances were difficult, I never missed paying my tithe. And we never went hungry.

For the most part, I was in good spirits because we were free. Yet my burden of resentment grew heavier. I continued to resist God's nudges toward forgiveness. The more he nudged, the more I resisted. And the more my anger grew.

Why is forgiveness such a big deal, Lord? I serve you faithfully. I am at church every time the door opens. Doesn't that count for anything? Can't you give me a little slack? We're not talking about some spur-of-the-moment solitary act of violence committed by someone who was drunk or high on drugs. My dad was cold sober all of those years. He knew exactly what he was doing! It's hard to forgive someone who is that mean. In fact, for me, it's impossible.

And I was right. As long as I chose not to forgive, forgiveness was impossible.

HALF THE BATTLE

One day, I recalled conversations with my mom that had occurred frequently throughout my childhood. After asking me to do something, I had often whined, "But I can't."

Mother, who despite all of her disadvantages had never let the word *can't* stop her from attempting anything worthwhile, asked, "Why can't you?"

"I don't know how. And besides, I don't want to—it's too hard."

Her response was always the same. "Honey, wanting to is half the battle."

I pondered the wisdom of her words. Could it be that the heavy burden of unforgiveness weighing upon me now was not because of my inability to forgive, nor God's unwillingness to help me forgive, but because of my refusal to forgive? But why can't I want to forgive Dad?

Struggling with this issue, I realized I had misconceptions about forgiveness. I believed that forgiveness meant that the wrongs my dad had done would suddenly be okay and that he should not be fully punished according to the law. I also feared that as forgiving Christians, we would have to allow Dad access to us after his release, despite our fears and a lifetime injunction legally forbidding him from coming near us. After all, if you forgive someone, I reasoned, doesn't that mean you must not withhold your presence from that person even if you knew he would kill you?

I also felt that my refusal to forgive Dad was part of his punishment. I would get even with him by not forgiving him—which was about as logical as taking rat poison and then waiting for the rat to die. I thought my Dad would suffer if I didn't forgive him. I was wrong—I was the one who suffered. I'm sure he never lost one night's sleep because of my resentment. But I had. I had tossed and turned many sleepless, miserable nights because the poison of hate was working to destroy me.

But why hadn't God helped me? As I processed all of this, I realized that I had expected God to do something he would never do—wrestle me into forgiving against my will. I thought of forgiving merely because it was the "Christian thing to do," not because I wanted to forgive Dad.

Early one morning, before rushing off to work, I read with awe the words spoken by Jesus from the bleakness of the cross:

"Father, forgive them." As I pondered the words, I glanced out my window. The sun, shining through the treetops, slowly turned the dewdrops on each blade of overgrown grass into tiny diamonds. They danced in brilliant colors as a gentle wind blew lightly across the yard. Just as the sun turned those dewdrops into something lovely, God's truth began to illuminate the dark areas of my heart with new understanding.

As painful and as humiliating as death on the cross was for Jesus, I concluded, he experienced it because he chose to—not because he had to. He chose to because he knew what the benefits of his painful obedience would be for all mankind. It was love for the Father and each of us that had kept him there. Jesus was not a victim—it was his choice to be a sacrifice for us—and it was his choice to forgive. He wanted God's will more than his own.

My mind warmed as truth embraced it. God will always give us the power to do what will honor him, but he will never force anyone to do anything. Just as he hadn't forced Jesus to the cross, he would never force me to forgive. I must sincerely want to. But how?

FATHER, MAY I?

For me it was a giant step that morning when I decided to want to forgive Dad. I prayed, *Lord, please help me to change my want-tos. I'm being as honest as I know how right now. Due to the resentful feelings I've held for so long in my heart, I don't want to forgive my father, and I know you won't force me. Yet my love for you and my desire to please you is stronger than my heart's desire to hold on to my bitterness. You have said that you would help us do anything that will make us a better person—if we ask for your help. So I'm asking. Please help me to want to forgive my father.* This became my daily prayer.

I don't remember when it happened—weeks, maybe months later—but I will always remember how it happened. One day, like a gentle breeze blowing the sweet fragrance of honeysuckle blossoms through the still air of a moonlit night, a sudden desire to forgive my father enveloped me. The bitterness of my heart melted as I whispered, "I forgive you, Dad—for everything!" The cleansing tears of relief that followed washed away all of the rancid remnants of resentment.

Shortly afterwards, I also forgave those Christians in Texarkana whom I felt had let me down. Jesus healed the hole in my heart and peeled away the scab so I could again begin to trust. My painful experiences of betrayal evolved into a blessing, for I learned at an early age that there is a difference between trusting people and leaning our total emotional weight upon them. God is the only one we are to love and trust with all our heart, soul, body, mind, and strength all of the time, because he is the only one who will never let us down. If we lean too hard on others, we will likely fall down when they move by abandoning or disappointing us. In our disillusionment, we will become bitter and distrusting. Let's face it, we are human. Each of us will disappoint someone at sometime. We need to understand this and not be shocked when it happens. God understands this frailty of human nature, and so should we.

"Yet he was merciful and forgave their sins...Many a time he held back his anger and did not unleash his fury! For he remembered that they were merely mortal" (Psalm 78:38-39). We will never fall if we remember that our anchor is not secured by flesh. It holds solid and secure only in the spiritual—in Christ.

"This confidence is like a strong and trustworthy anchor for our souls. It leads us through the curtain of heaven into God's inner sanctuary" (Hebrews 6:19). I didn't know then that when I forgave my father, it would open my heart to an ongoing power— a power that would enable me to forgive him one final time at another tragic time and place.

LOVE'S BUMPY ROAD

Mrs. Chappell beamed as she hurried toward me following the church service. "I want you to meet my son, Jerry," she called out.

She had spoken of her son for months, but he had never attended any of our services. I was choir director at our small church, and quite a few mothers dragged their sons to church to meet me. I suspected they were dangling me as an incentive to get their sons to take a more serious look at their spiritual needs. Mrs. Chappell was no exception.

I rarely dated anyone who was not a Christian. I firmly believed God's admonition "Don't team up with those who are unbelievers...How can light live with darkness?" (2 Corinthians 6:14).

I knew that even the best marriages had their difficult moments, times when prayer and obedience to God were imperative to avoid the divorce court. My future husband and I must serve the same God, for how could I ask God to whisper his truths into my husband's heart if my husband's heart didn't belong to him? To marry a nonbeliever would be like trying to mix oil and water.

This morning, however, Jerry stood beside her, blue eyes sparkling, his wavy auburn hair slicked back. We shook hands, but no sparks flew. I told him I hoped he would visit the church again, and he did. He asked me out for a Coke following an evening service, and we began dating. He was kind and gentle and fun to be with.

Several weeks later, while playing miniature golf, we drifted onto the subject of our plans for the future. "Once my family can make it without me," I said, lining my putter up behind the ball for a short putt, "I'd like to attend a Christian college in Riverside, major in music, and become a music director. Oh, rats!" I lamented, missing the hole. While Jerry made his putt, I continued, "That would be a disappointment to all of my aunts in the South, though—they're praying for me to find the right man and get married. They say I'm an old maid."

"At twenty-two?" Jerry quipped, brows raised.

"Most of my high school friends married right after graduation," I explained.

Jerry laughed and said, "Well, you don't look like an old maid to me."

"I don't know what an old maid is supposed to look like, but I'll probably look even more like one by the time I do get married—which is a long way off. And my future husband must be a Christian." The last statement wasn't directed at Jerry; it was a matter-of-fact comment made to a good friend. I added scripture to explain my position.

"I know what you mean," Jerry said. "Marriage isn't in my plans for a long time either. I'm only an apprentice now, but soon I'm going to be a sheet metal journeyman, and I'll make more money. I want to save up and one day start a business of my own."

He ignored my comments about my future husband's spiritual qualifications. There was no point since there was no romantic interest in our dating. We both relaxed and enjoyed our platonic friendship, secure in the belief that it would never lead to anything romantic.

During the following months, Jerry attended church regularly. One night, God whispered to his heart, and he responded by inviting Christ into his life. The stage was now set for Cupid, whose aim was perfect. Jerry and I fell in love, but there was a problem. Jerry gave in to Cupid, but I resisted.

I wasn't consciously aware of my deep distrust of men. It was hidden deep in my soul, tucked away in a pocket of fear and incorrect assumptions. I should have noted the symptoms, but I didn't. Because of my background, I felt that God had somehow made a mistake when he created Adam. Oh, I believed that when Adam and Eve sinned, the rest of us inherited their disease, but

I felt that the male gender inherited a greater dose. Sure, Eve was the first to eat the forbidden fruit, but couldn't wimpy Adam have had the integrity to resist? Maybe if his character had been stronger, she wouldn't have been tempted. Thus, I suspected a serious flaw in the male species, a stronger genetic propensity for sin and violence that passed from Adam to all men—not women, just to men. I often asked myself, *Who starts wars, and who rapes, pillages, and brutalizes people? It's men! Rarely does a woman do anything so terrible.* Though my ideas felt valid, the root of my problem was fear. But I wasn't aware of it.

THE HARD-TO-SAY WORDS MYSTERY

Jerry and I enjoyed each other's company, and we laughed a lot. As our deep friendship grew, I relaxed, and love began to grow in my heart. Jerry's love for me grew stronger, and when he asked me to marry him, I accepted. Strangely, when he told me he loved me, I could not respond wholeheartedly. I was barely able to stiffly say the words "Me too."

Why is it so hard for me to say those beautiful and romantic words? I wondered. *What's wrong with me?* It didn't make sense, for I knew I wanted to be with him. *Maybe I don't really love him,* I wondered. *If I don't, then why am I so miserable when I'm not with him?* I couldn't sort it all out at the time, but one thing I knew—I couldn't imagine life without Jerry.

I was excited the following Saturday afternoon when we drove to a wholesale jeweler in Oxnard and picked out a beautiful wedding ring set. During our celebration dinner, Jerry placed the engagement ring on my finger and again told me how much he loved me. I responded with a kiss. I extended my hand so we could both admire the ring. The diamonds sparkled in the soft restaurant light.

As we both admired the ring encircling my finger, I stiffened with realization. A sharp feeling of bondage, braided into a steel-like band, looped itself around my heart and squeezed tightly. The suffocating depression I felt almost took my breath away.

Why am I depressed? I'm supposed to be happy, I wondered, shocked at the intensity of my feelings. I tried to shake them by discussing our upcoming wedding plans, but by the time we were in the car and driving home, I could barely breathe. I became quiet—very unusual for me. I curled up on the passenger's side and rested my head in Jerry's lap, so dejected I couldn't speak.

What have I done? I asked myself in shock.

I rubbed the ring, suddenly heavy on my finger, its significance now strangely unsettling. *This ring symbolizes a lifetime commitment. The same commitment that saying I love you brings,* I reminded myself. *You don't accept a ring, and you don't say I love you unless you intend to give yourself, your heart, your body, your entire life to a man—forever!*

I lay there, rigid with fright, as my apprehensive thoughts escalated.

How do I know he won't become like my father once we are married? Sure, he says he has turned his life over to God, but my dad made the same claims. Jerry is all sweetness and love now—he wants me to marry him—but what about later, in the privacy of our marriage, when there's nobody but him and me? And I wouldn't count! I closed my eyes, but I couldn't shut out my fears.

I dozed from exhaustion and had flashbacks to when I was eleven years old. After hearing Mom's screams early one evening, I ran through the open door into their bedroom. Mom was on her knees looking up at Dad, tears pouring down her face. Her raven hair was in disarray, most of it still in curlers. Dad stood above her, one large hair-covered curler still in his hand, roots and all. Mom's left hand covered the bleeding spot on her head, and through sobs she said, "One day I am going to hate you with the same fervor that I now love you."

Those words bore into my young psyche and branded my mind, never to be forgotten. At that moment I decided, *I don't ever want to love anyone that much! In fact, I don't ever want to love anyone, period!*

I was jerked back into the present when Jerry braced me with his hand as he braked the car, narrowly missing a truck that had changed lanes abruptly. I cringed at his touch.

What's wrong with me? I wondered again. As I lay there, hollow in heart, I didn't connect the dots. It wasn't until years later that I understood. All I knew at that moment was that I was suffocating with a feeling of oppression. Jerry sensed my distress. He stroked my face with his right hand, his left still on the wheel, and asked, "What's wrong, honey? You seem unhappy."

"I am," I mumbled.

After a long pause, he asked, "Are you sorry that we are engaged?"

I started crying. "I don't know why, but, yes, I am."

How those words must have slashed his heart! But he answered gently, "Then you can give the ring back to me. We won't make this commitment just yet." When we reached Santa Barbara, I took the ring off my finger and handed it to him. We hugged, he kissed me on the cheek, and left.

Entering the house, I felt free again. Like a butterfly that had just escaped its captor's net. My heart soared in freedom.

The following Saturday, Jerry made the long drive back to Oxnard by himself and returned the ring. The salesman said, "I've been in this business a long time, and I'm a good judge of people. I'm going to put this set aside because I know you two will be back."

THE ULTIMATUM

Jerry and I continued dating. I returned to my previously happy self, but Jerry appeared gaunt, sometimes withdrawn.

He laughed less, and the sparkle in his blue eyes was gone. One night, after returning from a date, Jerry and I sat on the couch talking. Mom, Chuck, and Chris were still out, involved in their own lives, and the house was quiet. Jerry took my hands, looked me in the eyes, and announced, "If you don't marry me, I'm moving to a suburb near San Francisco. Remember my friend, Dave, who lives in Daley City? He's invited me to stay with him until I find a job."

My heart sank into a pit of shock and fear. *How can he just leave? I thought he loved me.* But I kept silent.

"When I walk out that door," he continued, "I will walk out of your life forever. I love you very much, but I can't go on this way." He stood and walked slowly toward the door without looking back.

I sat there, disturbed by this new development. Once again, I had a life-changing choice to make. Would I let the man of my dreams walk out of my life forever because of some unexplained fear of commitment, or would I go after him?

Like a mute-but-seeing statue, I watched Jerry open the door, step outside, and pull the door behind him—but he didn't close it shut. I heard his steps as he walked slowly down the sidewalk to his car. "Lord," I cried, "why do I always have to make such hard choices? I don't want Jerry to go, but I can't marry him either. Yet I know things can't stay the way they are, it's not fair to him. Please help me!" That moment appeared frozen in time.

Finally, I heard God whisper to my mind, *You have trusted me in the past in every difficult situation, and I helped you. I will always help, but I won't make your decisions for you. You struggle with the decision to marry Jerry because fear holds you in bondage. I am stronger than fear, but it is your decision to reject the painful memories of the past that will set you free. Your trust in me will then have room to grow.*

I ran to the door and threw it open. Jerry stood at the end of the walk, stoop-shouldered, with head bowed. "Please, don't go!"

I called out. Jerry whirled around as I rushed up to him. Under the streetlight, I saw his eyes widen in hope. Throwing myself into his open arms, I exclaimed, "I will marry you!"

He held me for a moment then pushed me away. His hands gripped my arms. "Are you sure?" he asked, voice cautious, eyes intent as they bore into mine.

The urgency of the situation prompted the truth from my heart as I answered without thinking, "Yes," I said, "I love you." But Jerry would not hear those words again until our honeymoon.

Ours wasn't a long engagement, for a month later we were married. Maybe it was because neither of us wanted to give me time to back out again. During the month's flurry of wedding preparations, I still couldn't tell Jerry I loved him. Though he didn't understand any more than I did why I couldn't say those words, he was patient. He knew I loved him even if I couldn't express it. Besides, he too was trusting his heavenly Father.

After the wedding, however, and on our honeymoon, it was a different story. Because Jerry and I were now truly one, both loving and trusting our future to the same God, I relaxed. I constantly showered Jerry with kisses and repeated over and over, "I love you. I love you!" I said it so often it almost drove him crazy.

"Okay, okay," he said one day, laughing, "I know you love me!"

But I was making up for lost time.

Almost two years later, our son David was born. Four years later, after experiencing the heartbreak of three miscarriages, one resulting in a burial, we were finally blessed with our beautiful daughter, Tamara. Life was good, and we were happy.

CUPID VISITS THE REST OF THE FAMILY

My sister Chris married, and our brother Chuck married. After dating Ira, her supervisor at work, Mom announced their engagement. Ira was a handsome former air force pilot who possessed all of the qualities that our father lacked. Six months later, they married.

We were happy for Mom. We prayed that her marriage would derail her bitterness. Though Cupid's arrow was firm and straight, it could not penetrate the inner core of hate at the center of Mom's heart. Her obsession over her past abuse by our father grew with each passing year. She felt betrayed by us children, who had each forgiven our father and released our painful past.

"How on earth could you forgive Clyde Caudle?" (Mom refused to refer to Dad as our father.) "Have you forgotten what he did to me? He tried to beat me to death with a claw hammer—remember!"

"I know, Mom," I often said, giving her a hug. "How could we ever forget something so terrible? We forgave Dad because we want to be free of him. You are still his prisoner because your hate keeps him in your thoughts day and night. You may as well still be with him."

No amount of reasoning from us children could convince Mother of the wisdom of forgiveness. We redoubled our expressions of love to her and intensified our prayers in her behalf. Every irritant that Mom experienced in life, however, was blamed upon our father, who thankfully had not reappeared. But the time was fast approaching when he would reenter the lives of his children.

GOD'S MYSTERIOUS WAYS

One day I met Joan Englander in our little town of Ojai, California. She was a reporter for a weekly column in our local newspaper. I realized later that God had directed our conversation, for she picked up on something I said and asked, "You have domestic abuse in your background?"

Surprised at her question, I nodded yes.

"How is that you are so loving, accepting, and outgoing when you come from a bad environment?"

"I never really thought about it. I...I g...guess it's because I'm a Christian," I stammered.

I rarely reflected on my past. I considered myself a positive person, and I believed my past was negative. Besides, I had forgiven my father and felt there was no need to think about my childhood, much less mention it. Most of my friends were unaware of my background, and I saw no reason for them to know. I was surprised that I had said anything to Joan that alluded to it.

I wasn't aware of it at the time, but I still carried deep feelings of shame. As a young child, we had lived on the other side of the tracks. We were considered by some to be riffraff, white trash. To me, my father's abuse of us merely confirmed those labels. I was afraid that if anyone learned about my background they would lose respect for me.

Feelings of guilt can be dealt with through repentance, forgiveness, and release, but shame is not so easily addressed. It wraps itself subtly around our psyche and whispers that we are of less value than others. Silence about my painful childhood only fertilized my feelings of shame, which grew best in darkness, away from God's light of truth. When God brought Joan into my life, he set into motion a chain of events that freed me from my chains of shame and affected the events of not only my life, but countless thousands thereafter.

Joan said she wanted to write a story for her column about my background of abuse and how I overcame it, but I was reluctant.

"Why would you want to write a story about me?"

"Because only God could have taken away your fear and replaced it with such powerful love. This is a miracle that has to be told! Statistics regarding abuse victims clearly show that your story isn't typical—it's out of the ordinary." I stared at her, without comprehension. "Most individuals who suffer abuse grow up to either marry someone who abuses them or they abuse their spouse and children, they take drugs or alcohol or become victims of prostitution. And when they have children, the process starts all over again. You see, abuse is a vicious cycle that is often carried from generation to generation. But you beat the odds! The world needs to know what God has done in your life."

Statistics had always impressed me, so I gave her request serious consideration. After struggling with the idea, I talked it over with Jerry, and we prayed about it. Maybe deep inside I hoped he would be against it, but he said, "Whatever you feel led to do, honey. It's your choice."

At last, I fearfully consented to a story, but I asked to remain anonymous.

"That's not possible," Joan explained. "I only do personal interviews." So I again relented. Midway through the interview, Joan stopped taking notes and looked at me, visibly moved. Tears slipped from her eyes as she said, "God is going to use this story to touch countless lives!"

I had no doubt that God would use Joan's article, for by this time I was convinced that was why she and I had met.

Following the interview, Joan said she needed an accompanying photo for the article. I balked. I had hoped that only a few people would read my story, but with my picture included, everyone I knew would see it and be sure to read the article.

"Why do you want a picture?" I groaned.

"Because you don't look like the typical victim. There is a glow, a radiance about you that the world needs to see."

Though I didn't understand the point she labored to make, I finally relented. But I was nervous. I prayed, "Lord, I know you are orchestrating all of this. So please help me to overcome my feelings of shame and not be afraid of what people might think. Help me to trust you to use my story any way you want."

Meanwhile, Joan worried. Titles for her articles were selected by the senior editor who had a propensity for using sensational headlines.

She waited anxiously for the first press run.

A short while later, a subdued Joan appeared at my door with several newspaper copies. I just hope," she said, chewing her lip, "that you're not offended by the title. I was afraid this might happen," she said, shaking her head.

I flipped the paper over to the back page to her column. At first I was shocked by the bold title glaring at me from the page. Then I was struck by the sudden realization that although Joan had no control over the title selection, God did. And he had a sense of humor! I laughed and said, "The title is perfect."

When I later showed the article to Jerry, however, he saw no humor in its title. He was angry. "Everyone is going to think I abuse you!"

"But not for long," I said, laughing. "It's obvious that God wants exposure for his power through this article, and he's going to get it!"

Holding the paper up again for Jerry to see, I pointed to the offensive headline and exclaimed, "There is not one person in this entire small valley who will see my picture below this title and not read every word—*Battered Woman Tells Story*. And I was right. Everyone I knew was stunned by the article.

The reaction of our dear friend Ferd Sobol was typical. With eyes crinkled in humor and voice tinged in admiration, he took my hands, looked into my eyes, and said, "Kitty, Kitty, Kitty—I had no idea you came from such a rough background. I always thought of you as just a sweet and smiling, pretty, plastic lady who was born with a silver spoon in her mouth. But you are one tough lady with real substance! I am impressed."

I was not offended by his candor. I cherished his response, for it was evidence that God knew what he was doing. This article showed the truth of God's power in a person's life. And with an added benefit for me—I was no longer ashamed.

After reading that story, my friend, Gerry King, who was an area representative for Stonecroft Ministries, invited me to a speaker's workshop in Ventura, California. From there, I became a speaker at Christian Women's Club luncheons and after-five dinner meetings, where for over twenty-nine years I have told countless women the good news that they too can become overcomers.

Several years later, following a luncheon one day, an attractive young woman approached me with a question. "Have you seen your father since his release from prison?"

"No," I answered.

"Then how do you know you have really forgiven him? You might feel differently if you were to see him again."

I knew I had forgiven Dad, but I wasn't sure how I would feel if I saw him again face-to-face. The validity of my forgiveness would be tested only one year later.

THE TEST

We hadn't seen Dad in thirty years when he contacted my brother, Chuck. Dad was remarried and had a married son. We were surprised to learn that our father and his wife, Mary, lived in our state. After great deliberation, Chuck and his wife, Nancy, took their family to visit Dad and Mary. Following that visit, Dad began corresponding with Chris and me, begging us to also visit him. But we were reluctant.

"Do you think we can trust him?" Chris asked.

"I don't know," I said, shaking my head. "In his letters he swears that he has changed. But I'd love to know how he's been treating his second family."

"I'm not sure I want to know," Chris said, shivering. Chuck wasn't too sure, either," she added. "Remember? When he visited Dad the first time, he went alone to check things out before taking his family."

"Well, Dad hasn't bothered us all of these years, so maybe he has changed," I said hopefully.

At Dad's insistence, we finally agreed to visit him. One Saturday morning, Jerry and I, with Chris and her husband, Everett, made the three-hour drive to Dad's home in Southern California. We rang the doorbell and waited. My pulse raced, and I reached for Chris's hand. It was sweaty, as was mine.

Dad opened the door, flashed us a nervous smile, and hesitated for a moment. His cold blue eyes, now a little paler, darted from Chris to me.

He looked the same, only older. He was still very trim, but his sandy-brown hair appeared dyed, and his face looked as though it had recently undergone a chemical peel. *He seems shorter!* I thought. *Somehow his 5'6"height had appeared much taller when we were children and he loomed over us as a monster.*

Dad reached out and embraced us girls. We responded stiffly. He then shook hands vigorously with our husbands, who appeared instantly impressed by his winsome charm.

Dad introduced us to Mary, a tiny brunette only one year older than I. There was something strangely familiar about her, but I didn't know what. Sensing her apprehension, I ignored her extended hand and hugged her. She smiled in relief.

After retiring to the family room, Mary served coffee while Chris and I showed Dad pictures of his grandchildren, three for her and two for me. Dad's hand's trembled noticeably as he handled each photo, poring over each one. Later he brought out their family albums, photographic evidence of happy family outings with their son, Howard.

I leaned back in the overstuffed chair and breathed in the sweet fragrance of orange blossoms cascading through the open window. I relaxed as I listened to the soft voices of the others deep in conversation.

I can't believe I'm really here, I mused. Suddenly, the significance of the moment hit me. *This has got to be a miracle—to sit here in the presence of the man I once hated and feared so much that I wanted him dead, yet I feel nothing but compassion and peace! This proves that my forgiveness is real. Thank You, Lord.*

From time to time, I sneaked peaks at Mary's face, trying to read her expressions, looking for telltale signs of abuse but found none. I caught Chris doing the same, and when our eyes met, we shrugged slightly.

While the others visited, Mary invited me for a walk in their garden. I was glad for an opportunity to be alone with her. I soon discovered that Mary was a Christian, was active in her church, sang in the choir, and obviously loved the Lord. She was a sweet, trusting soul who knew only what Dad had chosen to tell her of his past. As I listened to her gentle voice, I suddenly realized why she looked familiar. With her dark hair, deep green eyes, and cameo complexion, she bore a striking resemblance to my mother when she was Mary's age.

As we walked, Mary said, "Your dad has been a good husband to me and father to our son. He may be demanding and controlling sometimes, but he has never been physically abusive."

She glanced at me, but I said nothing. She continued, "Before we were married, he was honest with me about his past. He told me about his one mistake."

"One mistake?" I asked.

"Yes. That time when he was sick and almost killed your mother." She hesitated, searching for the right words. "You know, because your mother was such a 'bad' woman."

Fiery anger flared within me. I wanted to lash out and burn this ignorant, trusting woman with the branding iron of truth. How dare she believe Dad's lies about my mother! But the Holy Spirit nudged me. *Why do you want to hurt her? She has done nothing wrong. She believes your father's lies just as your mother did.*

With great control, I said gently, "All I will say, Mary, is this: our mother was a good wife and a wonderful mother."

Mary opened her mouth to reply but held her response. Controlling her anger, she finally said, "Your father is very hurt because you children have ignored him all these years."

Now it was my turn to say nothing. We walked into the house in stiff, strained silence.

HAD OUR FATHER REALLY CHANGED?

Later, in the car on the way home, the four of us discussed whether or not we thought Dad had really changed. The guys felt sure he had, but we girls weren't convinced.

"I feel sorry for him," I said, "but I think he's the same con that he always was. I think he's just doing everything he can to snatch a little time with the children he once abused."

"I just don't know," Chris said. "But I'm inclined to agree with Kitty."

Our husbands argued in Dad's defense. "Then why hasn't he abused his second family all these years?" Everett asked.

"He took Mary and your half-brother on family outings and did lots of fun things with them. They certainly didn't look miserable and abused in their pictures," Jerry added.

"Neither did we!" I retorted.

"And he goes to church with Mary," Everett observed.

"Only rarely," I corrected, recalling Mary's and my conversation in the garden.

"But he helps out at the Forest Home Christian campgrounds up in the mountains—even donated a station wagon to them. Remember how proud he was when he showed us pictures of it?"

"Besides, if he hasn't changed, how has he been able to hold his violent nature in check all these years?"

Their comments, tossed back and forth, echoed my own mental battle. I admitted I didn't have an answer. Only God knew.

The following spring, when Dad and Mary visited us in our Ojai home, Mary appeared withdrawn and pensive. When we were alone, she asked searching questions about Dad's past. She knew I sometimes gave away tapes of my Christian Women's Club speech, which covered my past abuse and forgiveness. She requested a tape, but I politely refused. She persisted.

"Why do you want this tape, Mary?" I asked, finally.

She hesitated for a long time, then admitted, "I'm afraid of your dad. He is in the early stages of Parkinson's disease, and he is becoming obsessed with death. He fears gradually losing control of his life and then dying." She hesitated, unsure of how to phrase her words. "He's making strange accusations. Although he has never hit me, I'm now afraid he will."

"What kind of accusations?" I probed. But she wouldn't elaborate.

Just before they left, I slipped her a tape and asked her to hide it. "Both of our lives will be in danger if Dad finds it," I warned. She nodded in agreement. From that tape she would learn at least part of the truth about Dad's past.

Several months later, Dad plunged their car off a cliff in the San Bernardino Mountains in a murder-suicide attempt. Mary was thrown clear, but halfway down the car caught on a ledge. Dad suffered only minor injuries. While he was transported by helicopter to the nearest hospital, Mary described Dad's deliberate attempt to kill her and himself to the officers at the accident scene. Dad was put under house arrest and, following his hospital release, was jailed pending his hearing.

Mary called me frequently from a nearby pay phone during Dad's incarceration. "I think your father has our phone line bugged," she explained. "Besides, I don't want any record of my calls to you."

I told Mary everything about Dad's past, leaving nothing out. During one of our conversations, I asked, "Mary, what did you mean when you were at our house and said Dad had started 'accusing' you?"

"Your dad often accused me of having an affair—said he wouldn't tolerate another man enjoying his wife and possessions after his death."

My throat tightened, and my heart pounded with realization. "Mary, you've got to leave! Dad accused my mom of the same thing before he tried to murder her."

Ignoring my statement, she continued, "Since he's been in jail, though, he's been nice. Says he didn't mean to go over the cliff. Said he just wasn't feeling well. I think psychiatric counseling will help," she said, hope in her voice.

"Mary, listen to me. In your garden you told me how devastated Dad was by his prison experience and how he vowed he would never go to prison again. I now understand why he has held a leash on his violence all of these years. It isn't because he has changed, it's because he fears prison."

"No," she said loyally, "counseling will help. I can't believe he'd really want to hurt me."

"Mary," my voice shook, "he tried to kill you! That's why he's in jail, remember? He will try to kill you again, and the next time he will succeed! He'll use a gun—not a car."

"Then I'll just have to trust God," she said, sighing.

"We should always trust God, Mary, but he trusts us too—to use the common sense he gave us. You've got to leave!"

My efforts to persuade Mary of the danger she was in finally bore fruit, but to no avail. One morning, she called and filled me in on all that had happened since our last conversation. She said she had related to the judge everything I had told her, but her efforts to convince him that Dad was dangerous and should not be released were futile.

"Since your father has never physically abused me all of these years, the judge discounted everything you'd told me about his past."

"Excuse me!" I yelled. "You mean the fact that Dad was standing before him for attempted murder of you isn't evidence that he is violent?"

"I guess not," she said, sadness in her voice. With sudden crisp sarcasm, Mary added, "Your father's female attorney made a very convincing plea on his behalf! She said I was just paranoid because of all that you had told me and that you had a personal vendetta against your father. She told the judge, 'Mr. Caudle's foot just slipped, and he accidentally hit the gas pedal instead of the brake.'"

Mary's voice began to shake as she continued. "Then I spoke up again and reminded the judge how terrified I was at the lookout point. How, when Clyde got out of the car, he looked over the edge as if checking out the terrain below. He was assessing it, not admiring it! I related how nervous I was as I watched him. When your father got back into the car, I saw him deliberately put it into drive. Not *R* for reverse, but *D* for drive! I knew what he was going to do and I screamed out, 'No, Clyde, don't do this!' but it was too late. He jammed the gas pedal, and we went flying over the cliff."

I shivered as I visualized the terrifying scene. "What did the judge say when you told him all of that?"

"Nothing, he just smiled. Ignoring what I said, he shuffled some papers and was quiet for a moment. He looked at your father and said, 'You are released on your own recognizance, pending your hearing.' Though the judge was addressing Clyde, he looked over directly at me and added, 'Now, Mr. Caudle, don't you go and hurt anyone,' and then he laughed."

White-hot anger flared within me at the ignorant judge. *How could he make such an insensitive, stupid remark!* My shoulders sagged as I fought an overwhelming sense of futility. *Mary is never going to make it. She doesn't have a chance—and it's so unfair!* But my fear for Mary only refueled my determination to help her.

"Mary, there is still time to leave. Let Dad get his own transportation from jail. Let his cute attorney drive him home," I snapped. "But you…you should pack and leave. Immediately!"

"I can't. I've done all I can," she said, her voice edged in fear. "Besides, where would I go? If I went to my mom's house or any other relative, he would just find me, and their lives would be in danger. But," she added, a false note of hope in her voice, "I really think everything will be okay. Thank you for everything, Kitty. I've got to leave now and pick him up."

"Please call me when you get a chance," I begged. "I need to know what is happening."

"If I can, I will," she promised.

Hot tears burned my skin as they trickled down my face.

"I will pray for you, Mary, and I'll pray for Dad—that he will listen to God's voice and not do what I'm afraid he will do."

That was the last time we spoke. Six weeks later, when my father failed to appear at his hearing, two deputy sheriffs were dispatched to Dad's Mentone home to arrest him. There they found the bodies of Dad and Mary—dead from gunshot wounds.

WHY, GOD?

So there I sat at their funeral. My heavy heart again was tempted to ask, *Why, Lord?* But it remained quiet. It knew the answer.

I thought back to the previous day, when Chris and I sat at my kitchen table in Ojai discussing plans for our long drive to the funeral with our husbands. Visibly shaken, Chris had run out of words and sat mute. I patted her hand and said, "We will get through this. The Lord will hold us close to him and give us the strength we need. We just need to keep praying."

Chris remained silent. Taking a leisurely sip of coffee, she stared out the window. Large orange leaves floated gently downward as the huge old oak began an early shedding of its splashy autumn attire.

Chris turned her head slowly back to me. Fixing her sad brown eyes upon mine, she asked through trembling lips, "How can you still believe in prayer? I prayed and prayed. I begged God to speak to Dad and change his heart, and look what happened. What good does prayer do, anyway?"

It was my turn to gaze out the window. *Oh Lord, my little sister has gone through so much already!*

I wondered if she was thinking back to yet another tragedy— one of the darkest of her young life. Chris was eighteen, pregnant, and sick—not only with nausea but with worry. Hours earlier, she had watched from their car as her young husband, nineteen-year-old Tom Kotecki descended into the choppy waters of the Pacific Ocean. After waiting for over an hour for a diver friend to join him, young Tom decided to break the cardinal rule of never diving alone. Primarily, because he was motivated— he was going to be a father! They had no medical insurance, and Tom planned to set aside the money received for the abalone he got that day for the upcoming medical bills.

This cold, foggy morning, at a remote point on the San Simeon Beach near Moro Bay, California, they were unaware that a hurricane forming at sea would be heading straight for their coast. "I begged him to not go down alone," Chris said, "but he was determined. 'I won't be gone that long, honey—only a couple of hours—you just wait for me here in the car, and keep the doors locked.'

"Plagued by a heavy premonition, I was so frightened I began sobbing. But no amount of pleading, begging, or crying would convince Tom to not go. With his jaw firmly set, he gave me a hard hug, so tight I thought my ribs would crack. After a long kiss, he turned but not before I glimpsed tears of empathy pooling in his own eyes—it broke his heart to see me cry. I trembled as Tom began walking slowly into the water.

"Submerged to his waist, he stopped to adjust some gauges on his scuba equipment. He turned halfway around as though he were coming back, and my heart jumped for joy. My hope was short-lived, though, as I watched my strong, handsome, blond Polish giant, fearful of nothing, resume his descent into the waters.

"I waited and waited. Without a watch and no clock in our old car, I had no idea as to the time. Exhausted, I dozed off and slept soundly. Suddenly, I was jolted awake by loud claps of thunder. The storm had hit full force, pounding our car with torrents of rain. Wild gusts of wind rocked the car violently, threatening to lift it into the air and slam it into the ocean with me and my unborn baby in it. *Where is Tom?* my heart cried, ripping with fear. It was too dark to view the ocean no matter how hard I strained to see. Terrified, I huddled there sobbing and praying. 'God, please bring Tom back safely—and please help me, I don't know what to do.'"

Her first prayer wasn't answered, but her second one was. Passing motorists stopped and took Chris to the constable's home where Mom, Jerry, and I joined her later. The weather was too fierce, and it was too dark to search for Tom. Fortunately, the storm spent itself that night. The following morning, a beautiful and clear dawn broke over a calm ocean in the cove where a tragic scene unfolded as Jerry and the search party retrieved Tom's body.

I never had any indication that Chris blamed God for not answering her first prayer. Despite her broken heart, God's wisdom reigned in her mind. She knew her young and fearless husband, whom she grieved for desperately, used poor judgment by going down alone. So how could anyone blame God? She was amazed and grateful, however, for God's response to her cries for someone to come and help her—and the miraculous way it happened.

The wife of the motorist, who stopped to help Chris that tragic day, said she "heard" Chris crying and praying as they passed by on Highway 101. Despite her husband's objections that it was impossible for her to hear anything from that distance, even if someone screamed at the top of their lungs, the road noise alone, not to mention the storm, he insisted, would have prevented her hearing anything. But the wife's strong persistence prevailed, and they turned around and went back.

"I could faintly see off in the distance car lights traveling on Highway 101," Chris said. Though they were few and far between, I started praying that one of them would come to my rescue. I didn't know how that would happen for it was almost impossible for anyone to see our car, so far out on the point with a hill blocking most of it from view. Also, it was pitch black. *It's hopeless*, I decided, crying harder. But minutes later, I noticed lights turn off the highway in my direction. My heart pounded with hope and fear as I watched the lights come slowly up and around the hill straight to my car. Was someone coming to help or hurt?

"A woman jumped out into the driving cold rain and yanked opened my door. Reaching in for me she said, 'Honey, I heard your prayers, and I'm here to help you.'"

I was confident that through Chris's experiences she'd realize, as most of us learn, that not all of our prayers are answered the way we want, but many are. Sometimes, however, in the presence of new, painful unanswered prayers, the old ones will likely resurface to haunt us. Only God's grace can sustain us through those times.

Despite answered and unanswered prayers in Chris's life, the tragic reality could not be denied that she was a bride, a widow, and a mother all in the same year—at the age of eighteen. But through it all, God's grace and love sustained her.

Chris got up to refresh her coffee, and I was jerked back to the present. *You know her heart better than anyone, Lord. You've been with her through all of her tragedies and you are with her now—even as her heart again questions you.*

Taking her hand in mine, I answered her question. "I believe in prayer now stronger than ever. I too prayed for Dad—that God would send the Holy Spirit to him and remind him of his need to accept Christ, to let go of his stubborn will, and to give God the broken pieces of his life to mend as only he can."

"And what good did it do? He didn't answer your prayers either," Chris said softly through gritted teeth. Tears of disappointment pooled in her eyes, threatening to spill.

"But he did. God heard all of our prayers."

"How can you say that?" she gasped in disbelief. "It's obvious he didn't answer them."

"Chris, we can't ask God to do something that will violate his integrity. He gave each of us a free will, which means we are not robots. We can make any choice we want. Though each of us will stand before God someday and be held accountable for our choices, he will never force any of us to do anything. That includes our father."

"So how then do you think God answered our prayers?"

"Think about it. Why would Dad wait six long, miserable weeks to do what he planned to do all along? It must have been difficult for him, hiding in their house behind closed doors, afraid to venture out because of the neighbors' stares and whispers, having to think up plausible answers to any close friend who might ask questions. He could have gone home and immediately done what he ultimately did. There was nothing to stop him. Why did he wait?"

Puzzled, but eager for my explanation, Chris shrugged.

"I believe Dad waited *because* of our prayers. It was during those long weeks that we were praying and asking God to speak to Dad. I believe it was during that time that the Holy Spirit tried to convince Dad that despite every wrong choice he had made in life, despite all of the heartaches and pain he had caused, not only to others, but to himself, God still loved him. I believe that Dad was reminded many times that Jesus had already paid for all of his sins on the cross—all he had to do was repent and ask forgiveness. I'm sure Dad understood the Spirit's reasoning, for he wasn't ignorant of the Scripture. He had heard God's truth countless times throughout his life. It was that truth that Dad struggled against day after day until he ultimately made his choice."

Yesterday's conversation seemed so long ago.

I glanced again at the stark and bare casket with its single rose. *Oh Dad, why did you struggle so? Why didn't you just yield to God's love?*

ꝗ

Each of us struggle with our choices, good and bad. Our wrong choices are powerful vehicles that can propel us, at high speeds, headlong in the wrong direction until we crash into the immovable wall of consequences. As we careen from one bad choice to another, however, not only do we suffer, but innocent people around us also suffer.

I'm certain my father didn't always deliberately set out to choose evil. I believe that most of his choices were based upon expediency, selfishness, and his obsessive desire to control. Dad embraced whatever choice seemed to promise the results he sought. However, only God knows the havoc Dad could have wrought had he succumbed to all of his wrong inclinations. This is true of each of us.

How ironic that I too had struggled long ago with this same loving God when I thought the death of my father was my only way out. But because I made the right choice at that time, decades later I was able to pray for that same father who thought death was his only way out. My choice resulted in a new beginning for me. Dad's choice resulted in a tragic ending.

Because my choice led to life and not death, it opened the door for me to make another good choice, one that affects my current situation in dynamic proportions. That was the decision to forgive my father.

Had I not already forgiven Dad for his past wrongs, this current tragedy would have revived my burning embers of resentment. I would have relived in vivid detail all of the horrors of my father's past violence, particularly his gruesome attack on our mother. I would have become even more enraged, with yet another layer of anger wound bitterly around my soul. I would have sat at the funeral out of stoic loyalty to Mary, hating my father, glaring grim-faced and tight-lipped at the two caskets. I would have shaken my fists mentally toward heaven, demanding an answer to "Why, God?"

Instead, I sat in the midst of a double tragedy, not as a traumatized, hate-filled survivor, but as a victorious overcomer overwhelmed with God's sweet peace. Yes, I grieved over the tragic loss of sweet Mary but rejoiced in the knowledge that she was in heaven.

I felt compassion for my father and a bone-chilling sadness. I knew why this happened. Despite a lifetime of opportunities to make the right choice by yielding his life to a loving God, Dad had once again made the wrong choice—his final wrong choice.

Our hearts struggle with bitterness and pain when the tragic effects of wrong choices made by others are unfairly flung upon us. We wonder if we can ever overcome our heartbreak and rise above it.

The answer is yes!

But how?

PART TWO

CHANGING MY SELF-IMAGE

I was fascinated one day by a bumper sticker on the car ahead of me. It consisted of one question: Who Do You Think You Are?

Our identity is often wrapped so tightly in our packaging—our passions, professions, or titles—that we rarely peel away the layers and discover who we really are. Consequently, many of us experience an identity crisis when we suddenly lose what we feel makes up our identity.

A number of years ago, a friend of mine was married to a successful, well-known surgeon. Without warning, her husband of many years divorced her for another woman. Heartbroken, she confided to me, "I don't know who I am anymore. I've always been known as Angela, Dr. Brown's wife."

It has been said that the greatest psychological discovery of the twentieth century was the discovery of self-image. Each of us has a mental picture of who we are and what we are like. This image is built by our beliefs about ourselves and is our picture as to the sort of person we are.

As children, the picture we hold of ourselves is influenced greatly by the bold brushstrokes of our environment. Strong feelings, good and bad, are the strokes used to paint our self-portrait. These feelings are referred to as "truth."

IS THE PICTURE CORRECT?

Too often our picture of who we think we are is painted by someone else. My father told me I was ugly and stupid. I don't know if he believed that or not, but those were his words. I could have either accepted them as truth or rejected them as merely his opinion. Children, however, are incapable of objectively evaluating statements made to them by others, especially adults. Because these words were spoken by an adult authority figure, my own father, I embraced them as truth. *Why would my father tell me I was ugly and stupid if it weren't so?* I reasoned. His abuse made me feel inferior, and consequently my feelings validated his negative descriptions of me—which led me to accept them as the truth. My young mind reasoned that no one would deliberately mistreat something of value, so I grew up believing I was worthless.

Because my mind accepted this incorrect picture painted by someone else (someone of authority), my brain tried to automatically "prove" the image I held of myself. In other words, I subconsciously tried to live up (or down) to that mental picture. My misconceptions were not unique to my situation. Each of us is affected by what others think and say about us.

In his book *See You at the Top*, Zig Ziglar writes about a fifteen-year-old boy whose teacher told him he should drop out of school and learn a trade because he lacked the intelligence to graduate from high school. Victor Seribriakoff took her advice. He became an itinerant worker doing a variety of jobs for the next seventeen years. At age thirty-two, however, Victor discovered that he was not a dunce as he had believed all those years. An evaluation revealed him to be a genius with an IQ of 161.

Armed with that new startling information, Victor gained newfound confidence. He began accumulating knowledge, expecting and achieving different results. He became more effective and productive. Years later he had written numerous books, secured a number of patents, and become a successful businessman.

The most amazing accomplishment of this former high school dropout was his election as chairman of the International Mensa Society—which has only one membership qualification—an IQ of 140. When Victor saw himself differently, he started acting differently.

WHAT HAPPENS IF I DON'T
CORRECT MY PICTURE?

I recall a line from a television sitcom that caused everyone to laugh, including me. One of the characters said, "Life is hard..." He then hesitated. Every body movement and facial expression let us know there was more to come. We waited for the expected words of wisdom, some helpful hints of hope—for each of us, deep in the heart of experience already knows that life, at times, is hard.

I held my breath in anticipation. He finally spoke and said, "...and then you die."

In the context of the script it was funny, for it was totally opposite of what we expected. Yet many people function within that sad picture of life, and it's not funny.

Unfortunately, because of the incorrect pictures we carry, many of us experience death before we die. Our hope for happiness crumbles into dust and lies at our feet. Faith that our future will differ from our past dwindles and dies. We are bone weary, tired of trying because we are always disappointed. We even tire of the anger that once propelled us. We just don't care anymore, and we give up. We wait for death, but for all intents and purposes, we are already dead.

But it can be different. Our future holds promises of unbelievable happiness, fulfillment, and joy—if we change our picture. How is that possible? By using the gift God has given us to make different choices, choices that are grounded in truth—choices that will lead to life and not to death.

Think about it. Do you carry a picture of yourself that is not true? False ideas will keep you in bondage physically, mentally, or spiritually. If so, God has good news for you: "And you will know the truth, and the truth will set you free" (John 8:32).

THE TRUTH ABOUT ME

My search for truth had to begin with God's Word, which tells us that God is the author of truth. Every word of truth that has been spoken since the beginning of time originated with God. Even when his truth is mouthed by liars and fools and twisted by evil men to accomplish their goals, truth is still truth—and God is still its author.

We are in a position to be set free from the incorrect picture we hold of ourselves when we embrace this reality—that God exists and that he is the author of all truth. Centuries ago, the psalmist looked up and proclaimed, "Only fools say in their hearts, 'There is no God'" (Psalm 14:1).

We commonly describe a fool as one who is not in touch with reality. For years, I had lived out of touch with reality regarding my value as a human being. Getting in touch with reality required my looking at God. As I looked at him and began to see what he is like, I began to see myself as he sees me. In reevaluating my thought patterns and belief system within this new frame of reference, I soon realized how fortunate I had been that fateful night when I attended church with my Uncle Paul and in desperation had looked up.

In the first chapter of the Bible, God tells us that we were created in his image. We are not gods by any stretch of the imagination, but we were created with some of the characteristics of our Creator in that we can reason, respond, create, and communicate ideas. The psalmist recognized this and marveled, "You made all the delicate, inner parts of my body and knit me together in my mother's womb. Thank you for making me so wonderfully complex! Your workmanship is marvelous—and how well I know it" (Psalm 139:13-14).

The truth is, we are wonderfully complex, and we have unbelievable potential. Some Bible translations include the statement that we are "fearfully and wonderfully made." And, indeed, we are "fearfully made." Because God gave us the freedom to choose, that reality can be downright scary! We can make choices that will result in our becoming a bully instead of a blessing, a terrorist instead of a tycoon, or a menace to mankind instead of a miracle worker in the world of medicine.

"There is a path before each person that seems right, but it ends in death" (Proverbs 14:12). The good news is, God did not create us and then leave us to ourselves to stumble around helplessly. He knows the pain we will experience when we try to live our lives without him. We are vulnerable and inclined to make wrong choices. In the midst of certain circumstances, many otherwise decent people will make bad choices—kill, commit adultery, steal, and lie—choices that will result in pain for everyone involved.

I came to realize that I could never become all I was created to be apart from the truths recorded in God's operator's manual, the Holy Bible. After all, he did create us. Who knows best what kind of care and maintenance we need to get the optimal performance we need and want in life?

It matters not what we were like in the past or what current misconceptions we hold of ourselves, we can have an entirely new beginning and a new identity. But we can't do it alone. We need supernatural power to achieve this!

WE NEED A SAVIOR

You may ask, "Why do we need a savior?" Without one we can't have a new identity. That's because, as recorded in the Bible, we were born with a terminal spiritual disease called sin. What caused this disease?

In Genesis, the very first book of the Bible, we read how God created Adam and Eve in his image. They could think, reason, create, and have fellowship with the supreme God of all creation. God loved them dearly and granted them rights and authority over absolutely everything in their beautiful haven, except one item—a solitary tree. God established this tree as his boundary, designating what was theirs and what was his.

They could eat fruit from any of the other countless trees there in the garden of paradise, but they were forbidden to eat fruit from that one tree. The reason the fruit on that tree was referred to as forbidden fruit was because the tree was not theirs—it was God's. That is logical. Aren't we forbidden to steal anything from our neighbors, not only by the Ten Commandments, but also according to man's laws? If we take something that is not ours, just because we want it, there is a penalty to be paid.

The tree was there as a reminder that not everything belonged to Adam and Eve. It stood as living evidence of God's sovereignty. (It likely was a precursor to God's claim of his rightful share of a tenth of harvests reaped and money earned.) God made it clear from the beginning that this was *his* tree. If they crossed the boundary set by him regarding his property, stole the fruit from his tree and ate it, the penalty would be devastating. Why? Because their lawlessness would represent blatant rebellion against their Creator. The punishment would be costly and far reaching. And so it is.

God had planned for them to live forever, but that gift would be forfeited if they rebelled against him. They would be cast out of their paradise and forced to work hard by the sweat of their brow for everything the rest of their lives, and then they would die.

What part of this "no" to Adam and Eve is so difficult to understand? You steal fruit from a tree that belongs to a supreme power who has life and death in his hands, and you suffer the consequences.

It's human nature to want what isn't ours, isn't it? But it's not like we don't have a choice. Adam and Eve could have chosen to reason instead of reach. They could have reasoned that they had it made there, why rock the boat and risk losing their lives for fruit from one tree when they had all of the other bountiful trees in the garden and everything else they could possibly want?

But because they chose to listen to the lies of the tempter, who created doubt in their mind in the motives of their loving God, they rebelled and reached. When they plucked the fruit and ate of it, it was a deliberate act of rebellion against God's instructions. Oh, maybe that wasn't their conscious motive—to rebel against God (it rarely is), but the outcome was the same. And the result of their rebellion was tragic—not only for them but for all mankind.

That first illegal act was called sin, and that sin polluted the spiritual bloodline of all mankind. Thus, every person born since Adam and Eve inherits this spiritual disease called sin. That's why we are called sinners. You and I don't have to do anything terrible to be a sinner. We were born one.

Is it fair that we should suffer for something someone else did? No, but that's a reality of life. Our tainted spiritual bloodline is reality, and we can do nothing about it—except to accept the only antidote provided for its cure, Jesus Christ.

But that sounds so hokey, archaic, old-fashioned, narrow, and one way to our modern way of thinking, that today's world rebels at the very thought. But think about it. For simplicity sake, let's hypothesize and compare the polluted bloodline (called sin, which causes us to rebel against God) to the HIV virus which causes AIDS. When women who carry this disease give birth, their babies are born with HIV. Is that fair? These innocent babies did nothing to incur this disease, but reality is they have it, because they were born with it. And maybe the mother did nothing wrong to contract this disease. It was possibly passed to her by her husband, who also may have done nothing wrong such as be involved in a promiscuous lifestyle, but he accidentally got it when treated in the ER from a blood transfusion—but they still have the disease. Why? Because somewhere, someone made an unwise choice that resulted in contracting this disease. That's reality.

Let's hypothesize again and say a person was born with some unknown antibodies in his blood that could act as an antidote for HIV. This blood was so powerful that when only one drop was mixed with contaminated blood, the HIV would instantly disintegrate and all of the blood would be pure and remain that way forever with automatic immunization. Never again would anyone have to fear getting HIV. Don't you imagine that when word got out about this amazing cure everyone with HIV the world over would rush to get this antidote?

Well, Christ is the only antidote that can cure our terminal spiritual bloodline disease. You can read in the Bible the details of how it happened, but here is a brief synopsis.

Christ, born of a virgin but a son of God and sinless, sacrificed his life on the cross to provide his perfect blood as the only antidote for our sin disease. After dying, he then rose from the dead. This final act sealed the destruction of spiritual death forever, meaning that following death we will continue to live. That is wonderful news for those who accept the antidote for they will reign forever with God. But it is tragic news for those who reject the antidote. Although they too will live forever they will suffer for all eternity separated from God and everything good. So the key to a happy hereafter is the antidote Christ.

Does this make sense? Maybe not to some, but according to the Bible, it is reality. Fortunately, one doesn't have to understand reality to embrace it.

Personally, I still don't understand the normal arrival of a baby. Couldn't there have been an easier way? Why must it be born through pain, blood, sweat, and tears? I would have gladly chosen another option, had one been available, after personally going through that experience several times. But the normal method of arrival for a baby is reality.

I much prefer the fabricated story I was told as a child, which sounds much nicer. When I asked the age-old question about where babies come from, my mother gave this explanation:

"A pure white stork leaves a baby on a stump in a beautiful marshy area, with fragrant lilies and wildflowers all around, while bright-colored birds fly about, singing its welcome and announcing its arrival. When a couple wants a baby, they simply walk out into these lovely surroundings and look until they find their baby on a moss-covered stump."

How many times as a child did I rush to every stump I saw in a marshy area, hoping to find a sweet little baby? I was always disappointed, of course. But not nearly as disappointed as when I learned the gory truth about how babies really arrive!

Many fabricated stories are told about how people can get to heaven other than through Christ. Innumerable smorgasbord arrangements of appetizing choices are presented for the mind of man to sample as a means of entering the hereafter. Fables appear more palatable because they bypass the gross idea of mankind being sinners due to a terminal spiritual disease inherited through its bloodline—one that requires a specific antidote. These spiritual presentations are much more attractive than the story of Jesus agonizing through blood, sweat, and tears, and ultimately dying on a bloody cross.

The problem is this: all the other plans offer only expensive placebos while leaving out the real antidote. Strange, when you think about it, because the real antidote is free for the asking—prepaid by the donor, Jesus. Sadly, many prefer the fabricated fables equivalent to the stork and stump story, which aren't even close to reality.

But back to how God gives us a new identity—and why he would want to. It's because he loves us. He has from the beginning and always will. Even as Adam and Eve were munching on the stolen fruit, God was already planning the antidote.

The Bible is more than a mere operator's manual: it is God's love letter to us. Throughout this entire book he pours out his miraculous love to each of us. Have you ever read more beautiful words of love than these?

> Do not be afraid, for I have ransomed you. I have called you by name; you are mine. When you go through deep waters and great trouble, I will be with you. When you go through rivers of difficulty, you will not drown! When you walk through the fire of oppression, you will not be burned up; the flames will not consume you. For I am the Lord, your God...your Savior...you are precious to me. You are honored, and I love you.
>
> Isaiah 43:1-4

When we accept God's antidote for sin, Christ, and all of his resurrected power into our lives, we are also given a new identity and a new reason for living.

> Therefore, if anyone is in Christ, he is a new creation; the old is gone, the new has come. All this is from God, who reconciled us to himself through Christ and gave us the ministry of reconciliation: that God was reconciling the world to himself in Christ, not counting men's sins against them."
>
> 2 Corinthians 5:17-19

Wow! Talk about a new beginning!

God will change our soul and give us a new identity, just as he did for me the night I trusted my life to him through Christ. But there is one thing God will not do for us: he will not build our character. That is our responsibility. But how do we accomplish this? Where do we even begin?

GOD GIVES LIFE, WE BUILD CHARACTER

What we are is God's gift to us. What we become is our gift to God.

—Anonymous writer as quoted by Eleanor Powell

Working on our gift to God must begin with accountability. This begins with the realization that we alone are responsible for building our personal character. No easy task. Will God help us? Of course! But it is through the daily choices we make that character is built. "Choose today whom you will serve... But as for me and my family, we will serve the Lord" (Joshua 24:15). Our character reflects our choices. What does the word *character* mean? Webster's defines it as "moral excellence and firmness." Our nation was founded by God-fearing men and women who proclaimed the importance of character. Its foundation was built on the principles outlined in God's Word that call for personal accountability—first to God, then to people.

People in the U.S. enjoy a great number of freedoms. But with freedom comes responsibility. Many of us clamor for more rights, but what we really seek is more license. We have enough freedom; what we really need is more accountability.

Freedom is in danger of degenerating into mere arbitrariness unless it is lived in terms of responsibleness. That is why I recommend that the Statue of Liberty on the East Coast be supplemented by a Statue of Responsibility on the West Coast.

Viktor Frankl, *Man's Search for Meaning*

The ideal of character has suffered blows in recent years. Too many people, from the highest levels of society down to the average mom and dad, have displayed an abysmal lack of character. Sadly, we see little difference between the lifestyles of many Christians and non-Christians. The divorce rate is the same. More and more Christian women become unwed mothers. Some Christian women also kill their unborn babies. Many couples, young and old alike, who call themselves Christians live together outside of marriage. The young say it is cheaper than marrying since there are no legal fees when they split up. The old claim financial benefits because they don't have to give up their pensions. If character costs us any type of inconvenience, it seems, Christian or not, we dump it.

VICTIMS OF OUR ENVIRONMENT?

Some psychologists tell us that we are helpless creatures of our circumstances—captive victims of our past. We are led to believe that our thoughts and actions, which originated from early childhood experiences and lie deeply buried in our subconscious mind, can never be understood, and will forever control us. How depressing!

And how untrue! That was not in the mind of our Creator when he created us. God never intended for any of his magnificent children to just wither up inside the cocoon of a victim mentality and be trapped forever in an isolated, suffocating web of past pain. Unfortunately, many in today's society who believe we are victims of our environment consequently believe that we should not be held responsible for our actions. But what about reason and choice?

If we disobey God's commandments and break man's laws, are we not to be held accountable? If we are not responsible for our actions because of our environment, neither are our parents, nor theirs, nor anyone else who lives or has ever lived. If our nation continues down this road of "no-fault" crimes, how are we different from animals? Would we not then live in a "survival of the fittest" or "kill or be killed" animalistic world?

Sadly, the guilty and innocent alike suffer from this attitude. Year after year, psychiatrist offices and self-help groups are filled to capacity with hurting individuals who blame someone else for their ongoing discomfort.

Our first and most important step in the building of character is to assume responsibility for our actions. Responsibility, however, is more than mere acknowledgment of one's wrong behavior. Our prisons are full of people who admit their crimes, but they blame someone else. In his book, *A Nation of Victims*, author Charles J. Sykes points out:

> Paradoxically, this don't-blame-me permissiveness is applied only to the self, not to others; it is compatible with an ideological Puritanism that is notable for its shrill demands of psychological, political, and linguistic correctness. The ethos of victimization has an endless capacity not only for exculpating one's self from blame, washing away responsibility in a torrent of explanation—racism, sexism, rotten parents, addiction, and illness—but also for projecting guilt onto others.

There are times, of course, when blame-placing thoughts are appropriate. As a helpless child, I blamed my father for my unhappiness, and he was the cause of my heartaches. But as I grew in years and maturity, I began to understand that though my father was the cause of most of my problems when I was young, he was not responsible for every heartache I would experience for the rest of my life. Nor was it fair to blame him for discomforts that come with living in an imperfect world. Charles Sykes continues,

> Increasingly, Americans act as if they had received a lifelong indemnification from misfortune and a contractual release from personal responsibility. The *British Economist* noted with bemusement that in the United States, "If you lose your job you can sue for the mental distress of being fired. If your bank goes broke, the government has insured your deposits...If you drive drunk and crash you can sue somebody for failing to warn you to stop drinking. There is always somebody else to blame.
>
> Unfortunately, that is a formula for social gridlock: the irresistible search for someone or something to blame colliding with the unmovable unwillingness to accept responsibility.
>
> Charles J. Sykes, *A Nation of Victims*

God's Word has much to say about responsibility. God gives clear-cut personal, family, and social guidelines that call for self-discipline and accountability. And he offers wisdom.

> If you need wisdom—if you want to know what God wants you to do—ask him, and he will gladly tell you. He will not resent you asking. But when you ask him, be sure that you really expect him to answer, for a doubtful mind is as unsettled as a wave of the sea that is driven and tossed by the wind. People like that should not expect to receive anything from the Lord. They can't make up their minds. They waver back and forth in everything they do...Whatever is good and perfect comes to us from God above who created all heaven's lights. Unlike the wind, he never changes or casts shifting shadows. In his goodness

he chose to make us his own children by giving us his true word. And we, out of all creation, became his choice possession.

James 1:5-8, 3:17-18

But what about the bitterness and pain we feel when we are hurt by those who choose not to live by God's guidelines? Surely we can't be held responsible for those feelings. Despite how we may feel, we are responsible for dealing appropriately with our hurts.

Don't copy the behavior and customs of this world, but let God transform you into a new person by changing the way you think. Then you will know what God wants you to do, and you will know how good and pleasing and perfect his will really is.

Romans 12:2

What is the pattern of the world? "I don't get mad—I get even." "Payback time!" "Make my day!" God says we are not to respond as the world does. Through the assimilation and practice of God's words and the prompting of other Christians, I was able to forgive my father and get on with my life. I am emotionally healed. I live a productive life today, unshackled by neuroses and free of bitterness. Some may call me simplistic, but I believe our problems would be solved if we read the Bible, believed it, and sought the aid of the Holy Spirit to incorporate God's counsel into our lives. But most of us don't. That's why so many of us seek earthly counselors. Earthly counselors can help us with some problems, but only God can truly heal a life.

Of course, there are times when I struggle, argue, and balk at some of God's instructions. But I ultimately end up trusting his counsel. After all, he made me! The more accountable I am to

God, the more I believe and test the truth of his words, and the more evidence I accumulate that they are true. Then I trust God even more—a beautiful spiritual cycle that builds character from the inside out.

Yes, reason and choice are powerful tools given to us when we were created. When these tools are properly used, we can break out of our victim mode and overcome anything. When we partner accountability with forgiveness, there is a dynamic synergistic action that results in complete freedom.

When I stopped blaming my father and everyone else who had hurt me, I was amazed at the freedom it bought! You read correctly, *bought*, not brought. Freedom of any type is never free—it comes with a price. For the victim, the price is giving up the costly anger, resentment, negative thought patterns, and, possibly the priciest of all, a victim mentality. But it's worth the effort for the pay value includes a double bonus—self-respect and self-confidence.

In a world that shies away from accountability in direct proportion to its withdrawal from God, there is a greater need for each of us to be responsible for *our* actions—regardless of what anyone else does or says to us. If we assume the role as eternal victim, exempting ourselves of all personal accountability, who, then, will show the world how to overcome? The abuse cycle can and will continue to be kicked down the road. Tragically, statistics validate this reality as each generation watches violence erupt again and again, passed on by one generation of victims to the next.

When viewed as a whole, this problem might appear hopeless. Yet a greater reality exists—you and I *can* make a difference! Our bitter past, with all of its ugly baggage, need not be passed on to our innocent children and their children, carried forth like an Olympic torch. With God's help, we can and must demonstrate accountability in a world that perishes for lack of it. We can own our attitudes and actions and replace our negative liabilities with

the healing light of forgiveness—and that is a torch worth passing on!

A MIGHTY COUNSELOR

I once worked part time with a Christian woman who frequented her psychologist's couch. As a child, she had a one-time experience of sexual fondling by an uncle and was now heavy into therapy. During our breaks we had opportunity to get better acquainted. She appeared to be trapped in a time warp of victimization, unable to get beyond her childhood experience.

I asked if she had forgiven her uncle. She said yes, but her anger was apparent when she spoke of him. I gave her a tape of one of my speeches, hoping my experiences might help her. She returned it without comment, but I soon sensed her disapproval.

During one of our breaks one day, she announced with raised brows, "You are in denial about your pain. You put on the appearance of being healed and carefree, but you have never dealt with your terrible past. That's why you give speeches, laugh, and cut up so much. It's all a front. No one can come through what you did without professional help. You need serious counseling."

I understood her assumption. I had met people who were in denial, afraid to face the cause of their suppressed pain, living behind a facade. But they were survivors, not overcomers. I knew the difference.

"Jane, how do you think God has managed to help his children for over two thousand years without the aid of professional counselors? Has he just been fumbling along, drumming his fingers, waiting patiently for professionally-trained counselors to come to his rescue? God's power is not limited. Don't you believe God when he says that his Word is sharper and more powerful than any two-edged sword? And that belief, acceptance, and adherence to his Word can change lives? Despite what you think,

God has helped me to become an overcomer—and without the aid of professional counselors."

She studied me through her dark-rimmed glasses and opened her mouth, ready for rebuttal.

Not yet ready to give ground, I continued. "I would be presumptuous if I said that because I was healed without the aid of professional counseling, it is not necessary for you or anyone else to seek counseling. It is likewise presumptuous for you to say that it is impossible for me—or anyone else—to be healed without professional counseling." She closed her mouth, and without response, we returned to our desks in silence.

Why is it that we can wholeheartedly accept the scriptures that proclaim God's ability to love a sinful, despicable person, forgive him, give him a new heart and purpose in life, prepare for him a beautiful place in eternity, and yet balk at scriptures that promise his children the wisdom to overcome the negative actions of others? Does that sound reasonable—that Christ would die for the sinner and make all these wonderful accommodations for him and then neglect him when he suffers hurt after becoming a Christian? In Jane's defense, she had simply bought into the prevailing attitude of the time—that without lengthy counseling, all victims were doomed to a life of misery and dysfunction. She had also succumbed to the incorrect idea that "every family is dysfunctional and needs counseling."

VOLUNTEER VICTIMS?

Some years following the Emancipation Proclamation by President Lincoln, it was discovered that a number of slaves were still working for unscrupulous owners who never informed them they were free. Some stayed in bondage because they believed the emancipation news to be rumors. Yet others, fearing the unfamiliar responsibilities of freedom, remained on plantations where they felt secure.

Likewise, many abuse survivors experience feelings of heightened insecurity when facing the possibility of freedom. This fear of the unknown is often as strong as the fear of retaliation from the abuser should they try to leave and is the reason many victims remain in bondage—especially if they have children. Most uneducated victims have been trained to believe they are stupid and incapable of surviving on their own (as was my mother), that they have no value, and actually deserve the abuse they receive. Victims believe the toxic negatives they are mentally fed each day and doubt they could make responsible personal decisions. (How could they think otherwise—they've never been allowed to make decisions?) Consequently, many decide it's safer to live with known pains, no matter how unpleasant—than to venture into unknown territory that might hold even scarier problems. At least their known pain is familiar.

For however long individuals have been victims, that is how long they have thought and functioned as victims. In their situation they actually learned helplessness, according to Dr. Martin E.P. "Marty" Seligman, well-known American psychologist, educator, and author. Dr. Seligman believes his theory of learned helplessness is a psychological condition in which human beings (including animals) have learned to behave helplessly in a given situation—typically after experiencing some inability to avoid an adverse environment—even when they have the power to leave their circumstances.

Dr. Seligman noted a similarity with severely depressed patients, and maintained that clinical depression and related mental illnesses occur in part from their perception that they have no control over the outcome of a situation. (I often experience those same feelings when I have computer problems!) Dr. Seligman's positive philosophy teaches that individuals always have some form of control in their circumstances and teaches them to focus on what they *can* do and on what can go right, not only what can go wrong. By encouraging cognitive positive accountability he helps them outgrow their helpless perceptions.

(At this book's conclusion are reprints of five domestic violence articles that provide valuable tips with names and telephone numbers of organizations that can help abuse victims. These organizations, with their trained and caring professionals who are eager and willing to help, sadly did not exist when my family needed help.)

This condition of learned helplessness explains why many abuse survivors never develop into overcomers. Because they have successfully learned to live helplessly, they continue to live out that mental and emotional lifestyle even after they are free. They are so accustomed to living passively, that they abuse their precious freedom by expecting (and demanding) happiness from those upon whom they foist their power. They live in the past yet demand longed-for fulfillment in the present from those who can't provide it—children, mates, friends, society, and, yes, even counselors. Ignoring their freedom to pursue self-fulfillment and happiness through right choices, they find it easier to continue as they previously did—letting life happen to them while complaining bitterly about the outcome.

> If it's never our fault, we can't take responsibility for it. If we can't take responsibility for it, we'll always be its victim.
> -Richard Bach, Author

Personal accountability is God's beautiful gift to each of us. Our happiness and fulfillment is our responsibility and no one else's. When we choose to become responsible to our creator, ourselves, and then to others, we will be empowered to overcome all of life's misfortunes. This is God's plan for us—his only plan. There is no Plan B. When Jesus said he came that we might live life abundantly, that is exactly what he meant. Anything less is of our making, not his. To be overcomers, however, we must be wary at all times of the volunteer victim mentality. If not, we will remain in the cotton fields of mental slavery the rest of our lives and reap its harvest.

> What the caterpillar calls the end of the world, the master calls a butterfly.
>
> –Richard Bach, Author

MY WONDERFUL COUNSELOR

As a struggling abuse survivor, I didn't know how to solve my problems; I wasn't even sure what they were. All I knew was that I was miserable. But when I went to my wonderful Counselor and listened to him, my attitude began to change. This opened the door to healing. Who is my counselor?

> For a child is born to us, a son is given to us. And the government will rest on his shoulders. These will be his royal titles: Wonderful Counselor, Mighty God, Everlasting Father, Prince of Peace.
>
> Isaiah 9:6

My emotional healing took place not on a counselor's couch but on my knees before the throne of the mighty God—aka wonderful Counselor. Openly and honestly, I bowed in pain before him. In love, he listened as I daily vented my frustrations. He was patient as I questioned the wisdom of his counsel recorded in the Bible regarding anger:

> And don't sin by letting anger gain control over you. Don't let the sun go down while you are still angry, for anger

gives a mighty foothold to the devil. Get rid of all bitterness, rage, anger, harsh words, and slander, as well as all types of malicious behavior.

Ephesians 4:26-27, 31

God understood when I questioned the practicality of forgiveness. He held my heart together as I cried and debated the logic of praying for someone who was hurting me. He then blew his breath of love deep into my soul where he saw a tiny glowing desire to obey him, and fanned it into a burning flame of desire to closely follow his instructions.

My most important step in healing was the giving up of all rights to myself. I let go of my "right" to hate and seek revenge, to wallow in pain and self-pity. When I gave up these "rights," I found freedom.

Though not received in a professional counselor's office, counseling has played a vital role in my healing and growth. Each time I listen with open mind to a sermon by a godly minister, I am counseled. Each Sunday school lesson, presented by a godly teacher and discussed by class members, stretches my growth. I glean counsel from each conversation with a person who walks his talk.

And the impact made upon my life by God-inspired books, articles, CDs, DVDs, and Christian radio and television talk show programs can never be measured! I believe one of the single most important aids in my becoming an overcomer is a love for truth—God's truth, not man's opinion of truth. Truth is reality. It is our flawed thinking, our warped perceptions that prevent us from recognizing reality.

Truth exists; only falsehood has to be invented.

—Georges Braque

Many survivors live in a subjective world of feelings that has little to do with reality. Only when we see ourselves and our circumstances correctly can we take the appropriate steps to become an overcomer.

"When the Spirit of truth comes, he will guide you into all truth" (John 16:13). God is the author of truth, and the Holy Spirit leads me to its benefits. God's Word counseled me regarding what types of thoughts I should think. (Particularly helpful to me are the admonitions found in the fourth chapter of Philippians.)

Due to my negative background, I was starved for materials promoting positive and inspirational thoughts that called for accountability. I gorged my mind on books and tapes written by authors such as Robert Schuller, Dale Carnegie, Zig Ziglar, Victor Frankl, Adrian Rogers, Chuck Swindoll, and Dr. James Dobson. Rich is the counsel found in the book, *Telling Yourself the Truth*, by William Backus and Marie Chapian, and Joyce Meyer's *The Battlefield of the Mind*.

So have I been helped by counseling? Yes. God's truths from all sources help mold my character.

COUNSELORS ARE NEEDED

Of course, there are times when professional counseling is helpful and needed! But we must be careful in our selection of a counselor. He or she should be a God-fearing person who uses God's principles skillfully. We can't assume that every professional counselor who claims to be spiritual is a competent counselor. Nor should we assume that just anyone with a degree in psychology can help in every situation. For example, children who have been violently sexually abused should be counseled by professionals trained in treating that specific type of abuse.

The responsible counselor will concern himself/herself more with how quickly and effectively you can be helped to assume personal responsibility for your emotional and mental health than with how long he can keep you digging in the pit of your past pains—and digging into your pockets for return trips.

It is fruitless to keep rehashing the past, year after year, with no real effort at moving beyond our pain, since that keeps our focus on our victimization. Neither does it do us any good to seek the wise counsel of godly counselors if we aren't willing to follow their advice. It must be frustrating for competent counselors to feel that, in some cases, they are merely high-priced emotional babysitters.

Considering what I have said thus far about assuming responsibility for our thoughts, attitudes, and actions through obedience to the Scripture and my personal comments about never feeling the need for professional counseling to overcome my past, let me add a caveat. Some individuals are incapable of controlling their thought process without professional help. Many people suffer from chronic depression, bipolar disorder, or schizophrenia, including Christians. They feel guilty, believing their spiritual integrity is somehow inferior, and hesitate to seek help. Even after receiving professional help and proper medication, some carry the added burden of shame, feeling they are failing God and their Christian family in some way, since they aren't able to function at their optimum level without the aid of prescription drugs. Often parents don't recognize the symptoms of chronic depression in a child until it is too late. Some may suspect a disorder but attribute the symptoms to merely another stage of childhood growth. Or they could be in denial fearing if they sought help it would reflect on their Christian parenting skills.

"It is not a sin or a crime to be mentally ill," said my psychiatrist friend Dr. Prema Caruna, MD, during an interview. "Many of these diseases have a genetic biochemical imbalance component much related to many autoimmune disorders of a metabolic nature, for example, diabetes and thyroid dysfunction." Dr. Caruna added, "These conditions are usually not cured but may be controlled by appropriate lifestyle changes, stress control, and specific medication. Medically depressed people have biochemical depletion in their body and should seek professional help. When necessary, a psychiatric evaluation would be requested to rule out other physical causes and chronic conditions that could cause the depression with suicidal ideas.

"God has placed doctors and nurses in our lives. Their supervision, along with necessary prescribed medications, is often life-saving. In serious conditions, as mentioned above, an understanding for the need of medication compliance is absolutely necessary to help restore an individual and reintegrate a person back into society, enabling a productive life."

I asked Dr. Caruna for her opinion regarding times when a healthy individual may need counseling for a short period of time, without it becoming a long-term process.

"Yes. People can be temporarily depressed due to grief, loss of a person or relationship, or a divorce. Bereavement and recent trauma is helped with counseling, pastoral or lay or professional, for a limited period of time, so they can move on with help from family or friends. Sometimes medication is helpful, but only as a short-term measure."

Who among even the healthiest of us hasn't experienced anxiety and at times feared we were on the verge of "losing it?" Twice in my life I've suffered through those horrible feelings. As a medical transcriptionist, I'd typed thousands of medical reports and knew the symptoms of clinical depression. Most of my symptoms fit that diagnosis. However, I somehow knew I was not suffering from clinical depression, which my doctor would have treated me for with prescription drugs had I gone to him—especially had he known of my abuse background. He would have assumed I was prone to depression.

I began to suspect I was mentally and physically exhausted from pushing myself far too long to keep up with too many responsibilities without proper rest. I decided to temporarily add a natural mood enhancer to my daily regimen. My mild symptoms of depression and anxiety disappeared, proving my suspicion to be correct in my case. (I did check with my doctor prior to doing this.)

Undergirding everything we do to become overcomers must be a desire to put God first in our life, to absorb the truth of his words into our mind and soul and seek his guidance in everything. Bad things happen to good people—that is reality. We must expect it, face it, deal with it, and overcome it. If we refuse to adjust to this reality, we can do far more mental and physical damage to ourselves than could anyone else.

A PRISONER SET FREE

My friend Winnie Starnes shared how her mother was taken away in restraints by the police, kicking and screaming after the eruption of her years of silent hate for her insensitive husband (Winnie's father). She was taken to a psychiatric hospital where she underwent twenty-five shock treatments. She was released on psychotropic drugs and received additional shock treatments as an outpatient, but still no improvement. Her condition deteriorated until she was reduced to sitting disheveled in a rocker, staring out the window of their home in a semi-catatonic state day in and day out.

My friend was a Christian and prayed for her mother for two years. One day, she began reading aloud to her mom Psalm 107:19-20: "Lord, help! they cried in their trouble, and he saved them from their distress. He spoke, and they were healed— snatched from the door of death."

She asked her mother to forgive her father so she could be healed. She then began to repeat the passage Philippians 4:13, "I can do everything with the help of Christ who gives me the strength I need," to her mom each day. She asked her mom to believe it, to say it in her mind, and keep on doing that until she could say it out loud. She did this faithfully for three years, when one day, her mother suddenly broke free of her catatonic state and began speaking. She was normal again. Her mom said she'd been in a dark place, like a deep well, and couldn't crawl out, but the scriptures she heard were her lifeline. Light finally penetrated that dark place when she accepted Christ and forgave her husband—and was set free.

Winnie's mom began sharing her amazing story to women's groups at churches saying that for five years she sat imprisoned in her mental hell because of hate. When she let Christ into her life and forgave, God freed her.

But what about those who cause our pain? What is their role in our healing? An important step in overcoming is to realize we can never control others. Therefore, we must learn to control our own thoughts and actions.

Yes, it would be helpful if those who hurt us would assume responsibility, acknowledge their wrongs, and ask our forgiveness. But it isn't necessary. To say that our healing is dependent upon the willingness of the one who hurt us to engage in group therapy and bare all—or even to just one-on-one admit and accept responsibility for our pain—places us again in the hands of our tormentors. What if they refuse?

My father never admitted his physical and mental abuse to me, but that was his problem—not mine. Dad is accountable to God for his choices, just as I am for mine. Nothing he did nor failed to do can limit my reasoning power. And it was my choice to be an overcomer—not merely a survivor.

LETTING GO

I read recently there is an identity crisis everywhere. Americans are seeking to find out who they are, where they're coming from, what they're made of—and how they can lose ten to twenty pounds of it.

—James Dent, Charleston, *West Virginia Gazette*

We may not need to lose ten to twenty pounds, but most of us need to lose some heavy negative mental baggage. Letting go may sound like a passive thing to do, but it isn't. It takes courage, strength, and faith.

A climber fell off a cliff. As he tumbled down into the huge canyon, he grabbed hold of a branch of a small tree.

"Help!" he shouted. "Is there anyone up there?"

A deep, majestic voice from the sky echoed through the canyon. "I will help you, my son. But first you must have faith and trust me."

"All right, all right—I trust you," answered the man.

The voice replied, "Let go of the branch."

There was a long pause, and the man shouted again, "Is there anyone else up there?"

Too often we call out to God, and when he responds, we don't like his answer. We look around for some other source of help. But he is the *great physician*—who better knows our needs? Why do we reject his prescription for pain and refuse to let go? Because we are weak. Only the strong can let go and follow God's leading.

The strength of a man consists in finding out the way God is going, and going that way.

—Henry Ward Beecher

It doesn't take a lot of strength to hang on. It takes a lot of strength to let go.

—Rep. J. C. Watts, Jr., in *Time*

We have trouble letting go because we are all tangled up in our baggage. We want to get free but we aren't sure how. Many of us are trying. We attend Bible studies, read books, and listen to tapes and CDs. We are busy learning. But how long does it take to learn the principles that can help us change? Not that long. The only way we can shed the bad habits that keep us earthbound is to exercise the principles we learn.

Let's assume that you weigh thirty pounds too much, and you ask God to help you lose weight. You don't exercise, nor do you change your eating habits. But you pray every day begging God to help you lose weight.

How many pounds do you think you would lose? What's the matter? Don't you believe in prayer? God will help us do what we need to do, but he won't do it for us. Many survivors do not become overcomers because it takes hard work, and they are not willing to pay the price. A healthy, happy, proper mental attitude does not simply occur because we wish for it. We can pray for it, yes, but we must do our part before God will do his.

Therefore, since we are surrounded by such a huge crowd of witnesses to the life of faith, let us strip off every weight that slows us down, especially the sin that so easily hinders our progress. And let us run with endurance the race that God has set before us.

Hebrews 12:1

What is your weight? Not your physical weight, but the negative weight that drags you down.

WORKOUT TIME!

Just prior to my fortieth birthday I joined a gym. The instructor spent considerable time explaining my exercise routine and demonstrating the use of each exercise machine. She also stressed the importance of changing my eating habits. After observing my workouts for several days, she was confident I understood the routine and concentrated on other newcomers. I never missed a day, I watched my diet, and I worked out diligently. Sometime later, I noticed the instructor watching my every move. She walked over and said something I did not want to hear.

"I've been observing your workout—and you're performing that exercise incorrectly." My heart sank. "I've been sweating through this routine for over a month. You mean I've been wasting my time?" I whined.

"So far as getting the desired results, yes." She then showed me the correct way, stating that she had shown me how to perform that particular exercise several times when I'd first joined the gym. For some reason, I had slipped into my own way of doing it.

"When you do it like this," she said, demonstrating the incorrect way, "you actually exercise the wrong muscles. I'm surprised you didn't notice—that's why we have mirrors in here," she chided gently.

I set to work trying to do the exercise correctly. I soon discovered, however, it was difficult to change because the muscle memory went automatically into the wrong exercise motions. It took deliberate concentration to perform the correct movements.

Driving home that day, I reflected on a recent discovery. I was turning into a critical person. I hadn't paid much attention—it began so subtly, but I seemed to be getting worse. *Now I understand,* I thought sadly, *I've been exercising my brain incorrectly! I'm becoming good at finding flaws in people.*

It was about that time I had become interested in the power of self-talk—what we say to ourselves. I had just acquired a dynamic tape series by a motivational speaker friend who encouraged us to take control of our self-talk. One of the tapes challenged us to a thirty-day mental-exercise test. We were to select someone who irritated us—mate, boss, co-worker, friend, whomever—and think no critical thoughts about that person for thirty days.

At that particular time in my life, the person who irritated me the most was my husband.

I can't recall what first prompted those critical thoughts—a midlife crisis, dealing with two teenagers, financial pressures, or just the wear and tear of married life—or it could have been my own self-centeredness. Each day I mentally talked to myself about the perceived shortcomings of my husband. With each "discussion," my critical thoughts multiplied and grew stronger. And I disliked him more. I became concerned and took the matter to God.

"Lord, my marriage to Jerry is a lifetime commitment, and right now, I feel like that's a death sentence. I don't want a divorce, but I can't stand the thought of living in a loveless marriage for the rest of my life. Would you please help me change my attitude toward him? You helped me to forgive my father, so will you help me love Jerry as I once did?"

Now remember the example where we asked God to help us lose thirty pounds? You know, where we discussed how we must do our part by managing our diet and exercising? Well, we now understand that God would not answer my prayer until I did my part. That tape series entered my life at the perfect time, for it outlined my needed mental-exercise routine.

The challenge was to kick out all negative thoughts about Jerry (or whomever) for thirty days. Since "all nature abhors a vacuum,"

I was to fill the space my negative thoughts had occupied with positive thoughts. I was not to replace one unkind thought with one kind thought—I was to replace one unkind thought with ten kind thoughts! Ten good qualities that described my husband.

This is called the principle of dilution. If you take a glass half filled with cola and pour water into it until it overflows and you keep pouring, eventually the cola will be gone and you will have a glass of pure, clean water.

I had recently attended a seminar where this concept was vividly demonstrated. The instructor spoke about how we should concentrate upon something we want and not upon what we don't want. To illustrate his point, the instructor stopped and said, "Despite what I say during the next few minutes, I want you to use all of your powers of concentration to not listen to the ceiling fan."

Until that moment I'd not been aware of the noisy ceiling fan. How was it possible that I had not heard it before? His point was well made, for the more I concentrated on not listening to the fan, the more aware I became of it—and the louder the sound. Gradually, I became so interested in the new information the instructor presented that I literally sat on the edge of my chair, waiting for his next word. I was so absorbed in what I wanted to hear that my mind blocked out what I didn't want to hear. The noisy fan was forgotten until he again reminded us of its sound, and his point was further proved.

God created our brain as a goal-striving mechanism to help us achieve whatever goal we focus upon. That is why our thoughts are so important. We can study medicine and become a lifesaving surgeon, or we can study weapons of mass destruction and become a terrorist. The mechanics of the mind function impartially.

But back to my challenge. I soon discovered it would take longer than thirty days. The rule was that whenever you failed, you had to start all over again—from day one. I worked and worked and went two weeks without letting one negative thought get a foothold in my mind. I was ecstatic. The very next day, I suffered a major setback, and I had to start all over again.

"Oh, no! Lord, at this rate, it's going to be a lifelong task for me."

"Bingo!" said the Holy Spirit.

I finally made my goal. Thirty wonderful days without one energy-leaking negative thought about my husband! What amazed me more than that accomplishment, however, was how much Jerry had improved during that short period of time! More importantly, I had developed a lifelong practice that became the norm for me rather than the exception.

Of course we are not to use this practice as a form of self-denial—a way to avoid conflict when our mate or someone else has flagrantly violated or abused us in some way and needs to be held accountable. I'm talking about freeing ourselves of the plain, old nitpicking critical habit of looking for flaws in others.

FRUITS OF THE SPIRIT DON'T INCLUDE CRABAPPLES

But when the Holy Spirit controls our lives, he will produce this kind of fruit in us: love, joy, peace, patience, kindness, goodness, faithfulness, gentleness, and self-control.

Galatians 5:22

Who in their right mind wouldn't want to be loving, joyful, at peace with God and man, patient, kind, good, faithful, gentle, and self-controlled? And why don't more of us produce good fruits? Because we are not in the right mind.

How can we be loving while thinking hateful thoughts?
How can we be joyful while dwelling in self-pity?

How can we know peace while harboring resentment?

How can we be patient while demanding instant gratification?

How can we be kind while planning revenge?

How can we be good while entertaining bad thoughts?

How can we be faithful while living in disobedience?

How can we be gentle while harboring combative thoughts?

And how can we produce fruit of the Spirit without using self-control? The only way we can reap a bountiful harvest is to control our thoughts and feelings, but we can't do it without help.

> So I advise you to live according to your new life in the Holy Spirit. Then you won't be doing what your sinful nature craves. The old sinful nature loves to do evil, which is just opposite from what the Holy Spirit wants. And the Spirit gives us desires that are opposite from what the sinful nature desires. These two forces are constantly fighting each other, and your choices are never free from this conflict.
>
> Galatians 5:16-17

Living in the Spirit is not a passive existence where we just fold our hands and pray, waiting for the fruit of the Spirit to drop in our laps, like an overripe fruit, honors bestowed upon the worthy—like the gold stars we won for perfect attendance in Sunday school, awards for just showing up. The fruit of the Spirit are character traits, formed in the fiery furnace of daily experience. They come to us not as rewards but as results, developed through hand-to-hand combat upon the battlefield of our mind. Ours is no minor conflict, for we fight in a life-and-death struggle against powerful evil forces that seek to control our mind.

> For we are not fighting against people made of flesh and blood, but against the evil rulers and authorities of

the unseen world, against those mighty powers of darkness who rule this world, and against wicked spirits in the heavenly realms.

Ephesians 6:12

God tells us not only to struggle with our thoughts but also to take them as captives.

We destroy every proud obstacle that keeps people from knowing God. We capture their rebellious thoughts and teach them to obey Christ.

2 Corinthians 10:5

So think clearly and exercise self-control.

1 Peter 1:13

TRUTH OR CONSEQUENCES

We do not have to accept every thought that pops into our mind, nor do we have to verbalize it. Jesus recognized the subtle method of temptation through thoughts voiced by others. Let's consider what happened during a conversation between Jesus and Peter in the eighth chapter of Mark.

Then Jesus began to tell them that he, the Son of Man, would suffer many terrible things and be rejected by the leaders, the leading priests, and the teachers of religious law. He would be killed, and three days later he would rise again. As he talked about this openly with his disciples, Peter took him aside and told him he shouldn't say things like that.

Mark 8:31-32

Peter loved Jesus deeply. He experienced a sudden memory loss, however, regarding God's prophecy requirements when he tried to detour Jesus from the road to Calvary. The Scriptures do not tell us what Peter said, but I can only imagine what I might have said had I been Peter.

> Surely you can't mean this, Lord? You are the Messiah! What earthly good will it do for you to give up the cause now, at the peak of your career, and let evil men kill you? What kind of testimony is that to the world? I'll tell you— they'll think you're weak, that you're not who you say you are. Your chosen people are counting on you, and you're going to let them down? Get a grip, Jesus. This martyr stuff sounds good, but what will it accomplish in the long run? Can't you do what is right without doing yourself in?

And what was Jesus's response to Peter's rebuke? "Jesus turned and looked at his disciples and then said to Peter very sternly, 'Get away from me, Satan! You are seeing things merely from a human point of view, not from God's'" (Mark 8:33).

I don't know how else to interpret this Scripture other than to believe that Satan used Peter's mind to house his evil thoughts. And Peter, being an indiscriminate messenger at that moment, delivered it straight to the Messiah, without even questioning the message. Jesus loved Peter, but he instantly recognized Satan's sneaky tactic in Peter's rebuke. Jesus knew that Satan's goal was to keep him from the cross, and what better way than to use one of Jesus's own disciples?

Peter meant well, but is it possible that part of his passion to protect Jesus from the cross stemmed from his own personal ambitions? At that time in his ministry, Peter may have felt that he had not left his all to follow someone who claimed to be the Messiah, only to have his hopes dashed on a cross.

Since Peter did not test the thoughts that popped into his mind against the Scripture, they escaped through his mouth in the form of a rebuke. Many of us have that problem. We would like to follow the saying "Be sure brain is engaged before putting mouth into motion," but most often we are more apt to "open mouth, insert foot." We need to exercise caution when advising others as to what they should or shouldn't do by carefully assessing our thoughts on the subject before opening our mouth.

Likewise, we need to develop our ability to recognize satanic suggestions as quickly as did Jesus, regardless of how logical or well-meaning they sound. We have no way of knowing, of course, the motive behind what others say, but we can test our thoughts and motives.

How do we test them? Against God's Word and the Holy Spirit at work within us. The problem for many of us is that we are not well equipped with the Word. We rarely read it much less study it enough to test our thoughts against it. "I have hidden your word in my heart that I might not sin against you" (Psalm 119:11).

Memorization of the words is helpful, but even more powerful is the absorption of their truth into our mind. We can then live by the principles of God's truth even when specific verses can't be recalled. We can then test our thoughts against God's principles. If a thought leads us away from God, it is a lie and should be banished. We can't let one evil thought into our mental camp to warm its hands by the fire of our imagination. It will catch us off guard and destroy us. A single thought can produce feelings, and feelings can result in actions. What harm can one evil thought produce?

I listened to a tape in which the speaker talked of a man who was interviewed in his prison cell. When asked why he had committed his crime, he related this story: "I worked at a construction site where every day, children passed by on their way to school. One day, I saw this little girl. At first, I just noticed how pretty

Kitty Chappell

she was. Every day I watched her go by. Then one day, a strange thought popped into my mind, *I wonder what it would feel like to caress her.*" The man said the next day when he saw her, the same thought popped into his mind. And again the next day and the next. Until late one afternoon, when he had the opportunity, he raped and then killed the little girl.

What a tragic action resulting from a single thought—entertained and not rejected.

> Every thought seed sown or allowed to fall into the mind, and to take root there, produces its own, blossoming sooner or later into act, and bearing its own fruitage of opportunity and circumstance. Good thoughts bear good fruit, bad thoughts bad fruit.
>
> —James Allen, *As a Man Thinketh*

BUT I CAN'T HELP THE WAY I FEEL!

Just as we are to test our thoughts, we are to test our feelings. For surviving victims, negative feelings often occur from a trigger reflex. Sometimes, without conscious thought, a situation reminds us of a painful past experience and our feelings are triggered, and we aren't even sure why.

Even into adulthood, I cried when I heard a puppy whimper or yelp. This was triggered automatically by my painful childhood memory experienced when I discovered the bodies of our tiny puppies killed by our father during the night.

For years, I cried when a court scene appeared on TV or in a movie, triggered by my painful memories of Dad's trial. These were triggered responses, occurring instantly without forethought. Even though they had occurred spontaneously, conscious thoughts of resentment toward my father flooded my mind—the father whom I had forgiven. The most difficult problem we face in forgetting past pain is learning to deal with an emotional system that has been programmed a certain way for so long that our feelings can't respond appropriately on demand.

Following a luncheon one day, a woman asked, "How often do you have to forgive your father?"

"What do you mean? I forgave him only once."

"I forgave my mother for her drunken abuse years ago," she explained, "but sometimes when I think of her I get angry, and I have to forgive her again. Some of my friends say I haven't really forgiven her if I get mad when I think of her. And please don't suggest counseling—I've gone to counselors for years. What I need to know is why do I continue to get angry at her when I think I've forgiven her?"

"Were you sincere when you forgave her?"

"Yes."

"Are you sure?"

"Definitely!"

"Forgiveness is a choice and has nothing to do with feelings. Either we forgive or we don't. You say that you were sincere, so forgiveness for your mother is a fact. Feelings, however, are not always based on fact. They are real, yes, but they may have little to do with our present reality. Your feelings of anger were appropriate at one time, but once you forgave your mother, they became inappropriate. You need to reject them each time you feel them."

"But I can't control my feelings."

"Are you sure about that?" I asked. "Were you ever deeply in love with another man before you married your husband?"

"Yes."

"Did you ever run into him accidentally after you were married?"

"Yes."

"How did you feel? Be honest."

Her face flushed. "I was surprised at how quickly those old romantic feelings resurfaced. I love my husband very much and am happily married, but I was shocked at how I felt. My hands actually became sweaty with excitement. I remember thinking, *I'm so glad I had my hair done today.*" Embarrassed at her admission, she lowered her eyes. "I actually hoped that he still found me attractive."

"Those were natural feelings," I said. "What I want to know is, what did you do with them?"

"What do you mean?"

"Those warm, romantic, fuzzy feelings feel good. Didn't you revel in them, relive those past memories, going over and over them in your mind for months afterward?"

"Of course not—I got rid of them as fast as I could!" she exclaimed.

"Why would you want to do that? They were just harmless feelings."

"Because it's not right—I'm married and those feelings are wrong now. Besides, I wouldn't want my husband drooling over some old flame. There could be problems."

"So what you're saying," I said, "is that you controlled your feelings by rejecting them."

She smiled. "Yes, I guess that's what I did."

"We can do the same thing with our past negative feelings. Just as the romantic feelings can cause problems if they are constantly entertained, so too can old feelings of anger and resentment. It may be more difficult, however, to reject them because we've probably entertained them for years. We relive those negative feelings over and over, not because we enjoy them, but because we don't know how to get rid of them. Once we learn how, we are freed from their power."

"How did you do it?"

"I made a conscious decision to face them. I was tired of them controlling me—I was going to control them! So each time they popped up, I said to myself, almost angrily, 'I don't like these negative and resentful feelings, and I won't tolerate them! Yes, they were real and normal at one time in past circumstances, but things are different now because of my forgiveness.'"

She listened intently as I continued.

"For years I was a slave to resentment, but the day I forgave, I was emancipated, set free. I am free now because I refused to let those negative feelings return and drag me back into the cotton fields of slavery again. If you reject those feelings, they'll never return. It's really just reprogramming your brain with updated data—your forgiveness."

She nodded in understanding.

"On a different track, I find this technique also works with other negative feelings such as fear and anxiety. Try it. You'll be amazed at what happens when you get your brain to working with you and not against you!

"When we control our thoughts about our feelings, then we exercise self-control, which God instructs us to do throughout his Word. I believe if more of us followed his instructions in this area, fewer of us would be on tranquilizers and other medications."

ANYONE CAN DO IT

Shortly after we were married, Jerry and I hiked up to the old Fremont Trail above Santa Barbara, California, with my mom and a friend. We briefly relived history as we recalled how General Fremont led his wagon trains across that range of mountains. We stared, amazed at the foot-deep trail cut in solid stone made by countless wagon wheels, each following the other in the same rut. It was easier for the wagon drivers to ride in the ruts than to try to get out. Fortunately, the ruts led in the right direction.

It takes even greater effort to get out of a mental rut. Our choice of thoughts provides the vehicle that will keep us in the rut or empower us to climb out.

I was discussing the importance of monitoring our thoughts and feelings one day with a Christian friend who was a survivor but not yet an overcomer. She responded crisply, "Well, that sounds an awful lot like mind control to me."

"That's exactly what it is!" I said excitedly. Her eyes narrowed as I continued. "Would you start your car engine, drive it onto the freeway at full speed, and then let go of the steering wheel?"

She answered, "Of course not!"

"Why not?"

"That's obvious," she said. "The car would go out of control."

"That's my point. Most of my life, I lived out of control. I allowed circumstances and negative feelings to steer my mind. They prevented me from getting to where I wanted to go by driving me to places I didn't want to be. Then I sat there like a helpless victim, blaming everyone else for the spot I was in and complaining, 'Why me?' Finally, I am beginning to take control of something precious that God gave me for my use alone—my mind. If I don't control it, someone else or circumstances will."

Many people feel that the overcomers they know or hear about are unique, a cut above other victims who were destined to live in the pit. They are convinced that these overcomers are favored by God with a special gift or ability to overcome trag- edies. They suspect that the overcomer never suffered as much as they did, or they wouldn't be able to climb out. But that is not true. God never shows partiality when it comes to giving his grace, strength, and power.

Many of us have walked in our rut for so long it has become our comfort zone—our "Fremont Trail rut." We feel safe there between its strong sides. Sure, we are miserable, but at least we know what to expect—even if it is only more of the same. The familiar may feel safe, but it can destroy us. At some point, our particular rut may run us off the edge of the mountain. When that happens, for fear that we will crash below, we too often grasp any branch we think can help us.

We may cling to a habit that seems to temporarily ease our pain and numb our heartaches, but in the end it will destroy our health and relationships and detour us from reaching our potential. And it could destroy us. "There is a path before each person that seems right, but it ends in death" (Proverbs 16:25). The good news is, no habit or lifestyle is impossible to break once we make the decision to let it go—and seek God's direction.

But what if we see the need to let go but we are frightened? We suspect that if we are to become an overcomer, we must change our way of thinking, and that is scary. We have programmed ourselves to react, not act. The thought of traveling a new road that demands taking responsibility for our thoughts and actions terrifies us. The overcomer's road looks much rougher and harder than does the victim's passive path. And we are not sure we want to pay the price. Besides, we don't even know where to begin.

> So now the LORD says, "Stop right where you are! Look for the old, godly way, and walk in it. Travel its path, and you will find rest for your souls."
>
> Jeremiah 6:16

FROM SURVIVOR TO OVERCOMER: A THREE-STEP PROCESS

There are only two ways to approach life—as a victim or as a gallant fighter—and you must decide if you want to act or react...a lot of people forget that.

—Merle Shain

Don't let evil conquer you, but conquer evil by doing good.

Romans 12:21

To everyone who is victorious I will give fruit from the tree of life in the paradise of God.

Revelation 2:7

What is the difference between surviving and overcoming?
Survive: to continue to exist or live after.
Overcome: to get the better of, overpower, overwhelm, to gain superiority.

Can we survive tragic circumstances, discard the negative effects of our experiences, and go on to became gallant warriors? Can we overpower our hate and resentment and overwhelm the tragedies of life with love, forgiveness, and a superior healthy outlook? Yes.

THE SURVIVOR

Many people survive unbelievably difficult circumstances, and we are amazed at their strong will and tenacity. I'm sure you can think of several people like this. Surviving is a wonderful thing, but we can't stop there. Sadly, many survivors never become overcomers. They exist, but they don't live—not in the full sense of the word.

Hiding our pain inside where it can eat away the precious core of life is not living. Venting our resentment and anger upon others also is not living. Neither is it living when we rely on the continual sympathy of those around us. If we depend upon the short-term rush we get from pity from others as a permanent cure, we are headed for trouble. Some survivors become addicted to the "warm fuzzies" of sympathy.

My mother, once a vibrant and happy woman, became addicted to pity. Year after year, she gave daily pity parties where she displayed her emotional wounds. The problem was, in order to hold the attention of friends who had heard her story many times (and to keep them from running away), she had to embellish her story with new shock material, often fabricated. Such is the danger of a victim hooked on pity.

> Self-pity is easily the most destructive of the non-pharmaceutical narcotics; it is addictive, gives momentary pleasure and separates the victim from reality.
> –John W. Gardner
> Former Secretary of Health, Education, and Welfare

A certain amount of sympathy is helpful, but at its best, pity should be nothing more than a temporary balm to soothe our pain. At its worst, it is a dangerous substitute for personal accountability. We are not entitled to a lifetime contract of sympathy because of past pains. Thinking otherwise traps us in a victim mentality.

My mother was a remarkable survivor, but sadly, she never became an overcomer. One would think that Mom would have been bitter and hateful while imprisoned for twenty-one years in an abusive marriage. To the contrary, she was laughter, light, and love for us in our bleak circumstances.

Following Dad's imprisonment and our flight to California, we children wanted to enjoy our newfound freedom, but Mother wanted to focus upon her past pain. Mom was wise about caring for her health. No recreational drugs, no cigarettes, no alcohol, and very little caffeine. If only she had exercised caution about what she fed her mind! Plastic surgery restored Mother's beauty, and she began dating, but inwardly she was turning into something ugly.

Mom had trusted Christ with her heart and life three months before Dad's final attempt upon her life, but now she seldom attended church. That was understandable since she was angry at God. She felt he had abandoned her.

"Where was God when I needed him the most?" she snarled one day, eyes snapping.

"God was there with you," I replied. "How do you think you survived?" I asked, my patience wearing thin.

"Because I refused to die—I wouldn't give him that satisfaction! My hate helped me survive," she hissed.

"Yes, Mom, hate can motivate a person to live, but hate can also destroy you. God loved you then, and he loves you now. He's waiting for you to let him fill you with his peace—as we kids have experienced."

"Peace? God wants me to have peace? Then why doesn't he strike Clyde Caudle with a bolt of lightning? I'll have peace when he drops dead."

But Mother was wrong. Years later, following Dad's death, peace never came. She simply transferred her hate to others.

Ten years before her death, I thought Mom was ready to leave her desert of discontent. She told me that after listening to a Christian radio program, she realized that God had not deserted her when she was almost murdered by Dad.

"I finally understand that God didn't abandon me. He kept me alive that night, just like the doctors said. They called it a miracle. And all this time I've been blaming God."

"I know, Mom," I said. "It's easy to blame God. We blame him when others hurt us, and we blame him when we hurt ourselves. But through it all, he loves us anyway." I hugged her and added, "Someday I pray you'll give your hurts to God. He can help again if you let him."

She suddenly stiffened. "If by that you mean I should forgive Clyde Caudle, forget it. I'll never forgive him!"

And she didn't. But her choice destroyed her health and broke our hearts.

Despite the devotion of our stepfather, Ira Hayes, a caring husband for over thirty-five years, Mother found nothing for which to be thankful. She made his life miserable as she spewed forth hate for our father and anyone who didn't agree with her.

Hoping that a godly psychologist might help, we children suggested counseling. We were surprised and excited when she agreed. Our excitement was short-lived when we realized her only reason for going was to gain support in her battle to convince us that we were wrong in forgiving our father and she was right in not forgiving him. When the psychologist didn't say what she wanted to hear, she stopped going.

Could Mom have been different? I believe the answer is yes. She was stable in every area except on the subject of our father and the past. She held positions with companies in California that required intelligence far beyond her fourth-grade education. On her job applications, she claimed a high school education, but her performance level was equivalent to that of a college graduate.

Could God have helped our mother overcome her past? Scripture says he can. "Give all your worries and cares to God, for he cares about you" (1 Peter 5:7). "But forget all that—it is nothing compared to what I am going to do. For I am about to do something new. See, I have already begun!" (Isaiah 43:18-19).

We can choose to humble ourselves, seek and accept Christ's help, or we can reject his offer. But if we refuse, we will be the losers. "But if you rebel against the LORD's commands and refuse to listen to him, then his hand will be as heavy upon you" (1 Samuel 12:15). "Yet they kept on sinning against him, rebelling against the Most High in the desert" (Psalm 78:17).

The children of Israel were only fourteen miles from their promised land of rest, but because of their grumbling lack of faith, they wandered in the desert for forty years. They did not believe God could protect them from the "giants" in the land that he had promised to give them. When they finally repented and sought God, he led them into their land of abundance and rest.

Because Mom focused on her giants of hate and resentment, she too wandered in her desert for over forty years before she was taken into her promised land upon her death. Finally, she had peace—in the arms of her Savior who understood. The forgiveness he had given her so long ago was not rescindable. I'm sure they wept tears of joy as he embraced her in welcome. But I wonder—could some of their tears have been for her wasted years in the desert?

> I am the LORD your God, who teaches you what is good for you and leads you along the paths you should follow. Oh, that you had listened to my commands! Then you would have had peace flowing like a gentle river and righteousness rolling over you like waves in the sea.
>
> Isaiah 48:17-18

THE OVERCOMER

Why are there so few overcomers? Because few of us realize the power of the thoughts that fuel our minds. And even fewer realize that we have a choice as to the type of fuel we use.

Good thoughts and actions can never produce bad results; bad thoughts and actions can never produce good results. This is but saying that nothing can come from corn but corn, nothing from nettles but nettles. Men understand this law in the natural world, and work with it; but few understand it in the mental and moral world (though its operation there is just as simple and undeviating), and they, therefore, do not cooperate with it.

—James Allen, *As a Man Thinketh*

Simply put, if we are obsessed with thoughts of bitterness and hate, we will become bitter and hateful. If we are obsessed with thoughts of kindness and love, we will become kind and loving. We become like our obsessions because our thoughts become our attitudes.

Men imagine that thought can be kept secret, but it cannot…hateful and condemnatory thoughts crystallize into habits of accusations and violence, which solidify into circumstances of injury and persecution…On the other hand, beautiful thoughts of all kinds crystallize into habits of grace and kindliness, which solidify into genial and sunny circumstances…gentle and forgiving thoughts crystallize into habits of gentleness…loving and unselfish thoughts crystallize into habits of self-forgetfulness for others.

—James Allen, *As a Man Thinketh*

Mr. Allen has fleshed out for us the truth of the old Scripture which tells is that whatever we think, that is what we are.

ATTITUDES

Words can never adequately convey the incredible impact of our attitude toward life. The longer I live the more convinced I become that life is 10 percent what happens to us and 90 percent how we respond to it.

I believe the single most significant decision I can make on a day-to-day basis is my choice of attitude. It is more important than my past, my education, my bankroll, my successes or failures, fame or pain, what other people think of me or say about me, my circumstances, or my position. Attitude keeps me going or cripples my progress. It alone fuels my fire or assaults my hope. When my attitudes are right, there's no barrier too high, no valley too deep, no dream too extreme, no challenge too great for me.

—Charles R. Swindoll, *Strengthening Your Grip*
[Nashville: W Publishing Group (formerly Word, Inc.)
1998].) Used by permission.

Viktor Frankl, a distinguished psychiatrist and survivor of unspeakable atrocities in Auschwitz, a World War II Nazi concentration camp, had this to say about attitude:

The last of the human freedoms is to choose one's attitude in any given set of circumstances...Man is ultimately self-determining. What he becomes—within the limits of endowment and environment—he has made out of himself. In the concentration camps, for example, in this living laboratory and on this testing ground, we watched and witnessed some of our comrades behave like swine while others behaved like saints. Man has both potentialities within himself: which one is actualized depends on decisions but not on conditions.

Viktor Frankl, *Man's Search for Meaning*

As a youth, it was difficult for me to develop, much less maintain, a right attitude in my volatile environment. The Bible was my main resource for cultivating healthy thinking as well as motivation for it. As much as I feared my father and hated his abuse, I knew God expected me to treat him with respect because of the fifth commandment. Of course, I didn't respect my father, how could I? But when I felt frustrated, not knowing how to deal with him as I should, I went to my heavenly Father for help. I didn't always succeed at living out God's principles, but with each fumbling attempt, I improved. God also helped me to be creative.

It was a two-fold blessing when I discovered I could make Dad laugh with a silly joke or funny face. I began using this tactic to diffuse and deflect any potential violent outburst that I sensed was brewing within my dad. I became adept at playing a court jester or clown in the bull's ring. Though it didn't always work, it was well worth the effort when it did. Developing this positive way of dealing with a negative situation helped everyone, specifically me. It was far more beneficial than just hiding my doubled fists in passive seething anger.

Motivation is a big factor in maintaining a right attitude in any life circumstance. The truth was I wanted my father to experience the joy and hope I did through a personal relationship with the one who died for both of us. Not just so Dad wouldn't be mean to us, but because I sincerely wanted him to be changed spiritually. That fueled my desire to be my best no matter what happened in our home.

My father gave me few joys that I can recall. The most precious gift he gave me, however, was passed to me by a stranger I met just before we moved to California.

"Caudle is an unusual name," the man said. "Would your first name happen to be Kitty?"

When I said yes, he replied, "I was in the same cell with your father for several days while he was waiting transport to the state prison following his trial. I think you should know what he said about you."

My heart tightened in anger. I vowed I'd never forgive my father for lying and calling me a prostitute in front of a packed courtroom just to save his own skin. I was certain whatever he said about me in a jail cell wouldn't be good.

The man continued. "Your dad mentioned you several times during my time with him. The day I was released, the last thing he said was, 'I told you about my oldest daughter, Kitty—well—all I can say is if there is such a thing as a perfect person, she is perfect!'"

My face crumpled as I fought tears—this was not what I expected.

I thank God for this tiny window he allowed me to glimpse through to see him at work. Despite my countless failures, God used the purest part of my attitude to briefly touch my father.

While few of us will experience atrocities such as were experienced by Dr. Frankl, each of us experiences heartache. It matters not the cause of our pain; all pain hurts, and we feel helpless. What can we do when we feel paralyzed by our circumstances? How can we move past being survivors to become overcomers? I hope the next few chapters will help to start you on the path to overcoming past hurts, great or small, that are preventing you from truly living.

STORY OF AN OVERCOMER

My friend Linda Turkiewicz is an overcomer. She relates the following story of what she did when she was utterly helpless.

"Frederic, my husband of four years, jammed his gun to my head and sneered, 'Now we'll see how tough this stubborn German-Irish gal really is!' He pulled the trigger. I heard the empty chamber click. 'Don't you like Russian roulette?' he asked, laughing. 'Let's try it again.' Twice I had heard an empty click. I closed my eyes and flinched as he cocked the trigger for the third time, waiting for the inevitable bullet to penetrate my skull and end it all. My life began to flash before my mind's eyes. I had survived childhood polio and, despite doctors' predictions that I would be wheelchair-bound, had learned to walk again using braces and crutches. I met Frederic at college, and we fell in love and married. Though doctors said I couldn't have children, we had two beautiful miracle girls, Michelle and Monique. Life had been wonderful—what happened?

"As a lab supervisor at a busy hospital, Frederic worked long hours. He began staying away from home even more, volunteering to work extra shifts. He took drugs to stay awake, then other drugs to help him sleep. He began to change. At first the changes were subtle. Then they progressed until he became a stranger—a stranger who was now trying to kill me.

"The gun clicked a third time. Again, an empty chamber. I opened my eyes as he suddenly lowered the gun. Without a word, he turned, walked into his bedroom, and shut the door.

"The next morning, Frederic was gone. We didn't know it then, but we would not hear from him for seventeen years. I did know, however, that it was up to me to get a job and raise my girls. I found work at a local hospital and eventually became administrator to several medical clinics in Scottsdale, Arizona. Finally, life was good again.

"Then one day, while I was riding with a friend, a drunken driver ran a red light and broadsided our car on the passenger side. I had severe head wounds and facial lacerations that would require plastic surgery. Worse yet, I suffered severe injuries to my sternum area and to both arms. I could no longer use crutches, and because my legs were useless, I was confined to a wheelchair—just as the doctors had predicted when I was eight years old.

"I couldn't drive and had to be transported everywhere. I was dependent upon others. Suddenly, this tough German-Irish gal was helpless and without hope. I knew I couldn't overcome this by myself. And was I angry! *Why me, God? Haven't I always taken care of myself? And haven't I been a good moral person?* But God didn't answer.

"One day my demands gave way to pleas for help. *Please, God, help me. I can't make it alone.* This time, God answered. He flooded my life with loving Christians. They took me to church, to Christian Women's Club luncheons, and finally to a women's retreat where I yielded my life to Christ as my Savior and Lord. I was no longer alone. I even forgave Frederic and was freed from resentment."

For over thirty-three years, Linda has been involved in directing various children's ministries. Currently she is director of a children's ministry in Tempe, Arizona. Linda is a dynamic overcomer—she says, not because she is a tough German-Irish gal survivor, but because she trusted God.

THE OVERCOMER'S JOURNEY: A THREE-STEP PROCESS

We have learned the difference between survivors and overcomers. We have read true stories of overcomers. We will now take a closer, in-depth look at the attitude of an overcomer.

The personal experiences and growth patterns of all overcomers are varied, but I believe the three steps listed below will enable anyone to overcome anything—even the most tragic circumstances in life—and emerge as a living marvel. There can be no lovelier gift to give back to our heavenly Father.

> My life is an example to many, because you have been my strength and protection. That is why I can never stop praising you; I declare your glory all day long.
>
> Psalms 71:7-8

Below, in a nutshell, is the three-step process from survivor to overcomer.

Step One: Forgiveness
Forgiveness has three parts:

1. We must accept forgiveness from God.

2. We must offer forgiveness to others.

3. We must forgive ourselves.

Step Two: Accountability

We must assume responsibility for our thoughts and actions.

Step Three: Gratitude

We must cultivate an "attitude of gratitude."

The next three chapters will take you through the three steps in an in-depth way. Your life doesn't have to be a ruin because of the difficult things in your past! Read on, and find the positive, fulfilling future God has for you.

STEP ONE: FORGIVENESS

I believe the first and most important step toward a happy and fulfilling life is forgiveness—a threefold process. The first part of step one, receiving God's forgiveness, is imperative for it involves not only our present life but also our eternal life. But if we skip parts two and three of step one, we will remain mere survivors.

GOD'S GIFT OF FORGIVENESS TO US

The single most important act of my life was addressing my personal need for forgiveness by God. This was accomplished through my acceptance of Christ. (Remember, he is the only antidote for our inherited tainted blood line and our personal sins.) "Because one person disobeyed God, many became sinners. But because one other person obeyed God, many will be made righteous" (Romans 5:19). "But if we confess our sins to him, he is faithful and just to forgive us our sins and to cleanse us from all wickedness" (1 John 1:9).

I mentioned in chapter 2 how I took this first step and humbly asked God to forgive my sins. We Christians speak of "giving our heart" to Jesus, but we also give him at that moment our sins, our broken dreams, and our pains. We can't carry these burdens any longer, so we trust him to lift them and deal with them. He then creates in us a new heart. "Create in me a clean heart, O God. Renew a loyal spirit within me" (Psalm 51:10).

If you are seriously interested in accepting Christ into your life, let me tell you how easy it is. Just pray from your heart the words that are presented in the prayer below, or use your own words. Sounds too easy, you say? The truth is, God *does* make it easy for us because he's already done the *hard* part. It's our mistaken ideas that make it seem difficult. But whether my words or yours, make them sincere—straight from *your* heart.

Dear God,

I'm not sure I understand everything I've heard or read about you, but one thing I do understand is that I am a sinner and that Christ died for my sins so I wouldn't have to. I confess my sins to you and ask you to forgive me. Please create in me a new heart, for I want you in my life forever.

In Jesus's name I pray.

Amen

God not only creates in us a new heart. He does much more. He gives us new life and power by sending the Holy Spirit to dwell within us. Never again can anything overcome us. His Spirit helps, guides, and comforts us. When no one understands how we feel, not even our mate or closest friends, the Holy Spirit does—because he knows our heart. He even helps us pray when we can't find the right words.

And the Holy Spirit helps us in our weakness. For example, we don't know what God wants us to pray for. But the Holy Spirit prays for us with groanings that cannot be expressed in words. And the Father who knows all hearts knows what the Spirit is saying, for the Spirit pleads for us believers in harmony with God's own will.

Romans 8:26-27

WE MUST FORGIVE OTHERS

So far, God has done all the giving. He rescued me from my tainted bloodline through the fresh and pure blood transfusion supplied by Christ, he forgave my sins, he instilled the Holy Spirit within me to comfort and to guide me, and he is preparing an eternal dwelling place for me.

> There is more than enough room in my Father's home. If this were not so, would I have told you that I am going to prepare a place for you? When everything is ready, I will come and get you, so that you will always be with me where I am.
>
> John 14:2-3

What have I given God thus far, other than my sins and my broken heart to be made new? Nothing. What can I give him? A life that honors him. I must be willing to do for others what he has done for me. How can those who sin against me believe that God, whom they have not met, will forgive them their sins if I, whom they have met, won't? My forgiveness helps provide evidence that God will do what he says he will do.

It is easier to accept forgiveness than it is to give it. We make the act of forgiving difficult because we focus on the disobedience of the one who hurt us rather than our need to be obedient to the one who forgave us. Maybe we need a clearer understanding of why we are to forgive. We are to forgive out of love and gratitude to God because he forgave us, because he expects it, because Christ set the example on the cross, and because the Holy Spirit enables us.

But aren't there some sins so calculated, evil, and vile that it is simply not possible to forgive them? Ask my overcomer friend, Lynne Bennett, who shares her amazing story below.

BREAKING FREE OF THE WEB

I didn't want to hurt my mother—I loved her dearly—but she left me no choice. And maybe if I told her my horrible secret, she would understand my anger and even help me. *But what if she doesn't believe me?*

When I entered the kitchen after school, Mom was leaning against the counter—rigid, with pursed lips and glassy eyes. *She's had too much to drink—again.*

"Sit down," she demanded as I placed my books on the table.

"Why do you hate your father so much?" she yelled. "All you do is scream at him and call him filthy names."

My throat tightened as her scorn pierced my heart. *Why does she have to be like this?*

Our father worked on an out-of-town highway construction job and was home only on weekends, leaving shortly after Sunday dinner not to return until the following Friday evening. Because Dad was gone so much, my sister, Jacque, and I desperately sought his love and attention. Instead of giving us the nurturing love we longed for when he was home, our dad took advantage of us. Beginning when I was three and Jacque five, Dad seduced and entrapped us in his carefully woven web. Over the next eight years, he wrapped us in an affectionate cocoon of silence, luring us into hiding places where he robbed us of our innocence. We weren't the only prey caught in Dad's web. He also molested several children of relatives and neighborhood friends.

"Answer me!" my mother screamed. "Why do you treat your father this way?"

Angry and worn down from concealing this secret for twelve troubling years, I was ready to talk, but first made Mom promise to never tell Dad.

As I sat down at the table, my heart pounded. *What will she say? And how do I even begin?* With my chest tight and throat dry, I took a deep breath and blurted out the ugly truth. I'd barely begun when Mom lunged at me, shrieking, "You're a liar! I don't believe you!"

My stomach lurched violently as Mom stormed out of the room. My throbbing head slumped to the table as I sobbed, "I told you that you wouldn't believe me."

But the worst was yet to come. The following day, Mom repeated my every word to Dad. A jagged rip tore through my heart, and I feared I would die from the pain of my mother's betrayal. Any hope that she would help me if I told her the truth now lay dead. I was totally alone.

Like strong weeds following a spring rain, resentment for my mother sprang up quickly, threatening to choke the life out of me. As the months passed, I sank into depression so deep I thought I might lose my mind. I eventually convinced my mother to take me to a psychiatrist, who basically said my parents needed to be there, not me. But that would never happen. My parents would never accept any responsibility for my suffering.

Hating and wanting no part of my dad, I quit high school and left home. But my pain followed, drawing me into a life of illegal drugs, hard liquor, and promiscuous behavior. All I wanted was to be loved, but most of the men I slept with just used me until someone else came along. I decided no man would ever truly love me. With a hardened heart, I used and abused men the way they had used and abused me. And sometimes I even got paid for it. By my early twenties, I'd become, what I later coined, a marriage atheist. However, this attitude softened one cold day after wrecking my car in a blizzard.

Steve, the handsome blond insurance rep, melted my heart with his infectious grin and baby-blue eyes. As we stood there in the insurance company's garage, assessing the damage, I felt in my heart Steve would be my husband. Our attraction grew, and two years later we married. However, marrying a wonderful man didn't eliminate my issues.

Full of anger and bitterness, I often erupted into uncontrolled fits of rage, and I manipulated, belittled, and verbally degraded Steve. My relentless abuse hurled Steve into a deep pit of depression. Instead of showing compassion, I told him he was pathetic, which destroyed him even more. Before our first anniversary, convinced that Steve no longer loved me, I phoned a man whose advances I had previously ignored. We were soon immersed in an affair.

I had no church upbringing, but I sometimes cried out in desperation to a God I knew nothing about. Shortly after one of those desperate cries, a girl friend said to me, "When are you going to end your affair and make something out of your marriage?" By that time, I had cheated on Steve for nearly three years out of our four-year marriage. Though it was far from true, I quipped, "Well, I've tried everything I can think of, but nothing is working. Guess I'm just going to have to turn it over to Jesus."

Two weeks later, at the age of thirty-one, I flew to Las Vegas intending to seduce an ex-boyfriend named Bill. The Bible tells us that God knows the thoughts and intentions of our hearts, and although Bill had absolutely no clue of my plans, God did. But he had plans of his own.

Only minutes after sitting down in Bill's camper home, he surprised me by sharing how he'd become a Christian ten years earlier. My heart was starved for the truth. During my week there, I questioned Bill relentlessly about God and the Bible. While Bill enthusiastically answered my many questions, God enveloped me with his love, and I began to yield as he softened my wounded and scarred heart. Feeling safe with Bill, I confessed my ongoing affair. Rather than condemnation, he showed me compassion. Even so, he made it clear that I must get serious with God and stop the affair, but then came the clincher—I also needed to forgive my father. Tears streamed down my face. "You're asking way too much of me, especially forgiving my father. I hate him! I can't forgive him. I don't even want to."

Bill was patient but insistent. "I know you can't," he said softly, "but Jesus will give you the ability to forgive."

During my flight home to Virginia, I reviewed my week in Vegas. My plan had been simply to employ another futile attempt to fill the void in my heart with an adulterous fling. But God's plan changed the course of my life for all eternity. Flying back that day, however, I feared how Steve would respond when I told him of my newfound belief in God.

I didn't tell Steve everything Bill had shared about God but enough that it was obvious something supernatural had happened. We soon started attending a church where three months later, Steve also received Christ.

We began pastoral counseling soon afterwards to restore our marriage. In a one-on-one session with our pastor, I admitted to my adulterous relationship before becoming a Christian. He warned me that someday I must tell Steve or the lie would eat me alive. I asked him when I should do that, and he said, "God will let you know." The pastor did advise me, however, to wait until Steve matured enough in his faith to handle that kind of information so that our marriage would have a better chance of survival. But in my heart, I decided I'd never tell Steve. As usual, God had different plans, and three years later, when God knew the time was right, I did.

Steve responded as expected—with shock, anger, and questions. Finally he bolted out, slamming the door behind him. After hours of roaming the golf course in pouring rain, he returned. "I don't want to forgive you!"

I had been weeping bitterly since he left, and his icy words paralyzed me. Then he added, "But I know I'm supposed to...so I do. I just pray the feelings will follow." The feelings did follow, but it took hard work on both our parts to rebuild our marriage. We now believe it was because we obeyed God, even though neither of us wanted to—me by confessing adultery and Steve by forgiving—that God removed Steve's anger and blessed our marriage with healing.

But what about my father?

It was only two weeks after the miracle of my conversion that a second miracle occurred. I'd had no desire to forgive my father—my hate went too deep and the wounds were too many. But God knew forgiveness of my father was the catalyst for my healing. While listening to Christian music as I drove home from work, my chest began aching, like my heart was being ripped open and my entire body on fire. Then, as though someone else were speaking, I heard myself say aloud, "I do forgive him. I love my dad, I really do!" At that moment, God stripped away all the hate, anger, and bitterness that I'd kept locked inside for over half my life. He then filled my heart with love and tenderness for my father that I'd never known. Tears of release rolled down my face as God freed me from the curse of my dad's web that had held me captive since a little girl.

I couldn't wait to share this miracle! My parents, regrettably, didn't share my excitement when I called them. "Dad, I want you to know I forgive you for what you did to me when I was a child. I forgive you too, Mom, for not believing me when I told you about Dad."

"You must really hate us to bring this up again after all these years!" Dad raged. "Why don't you just let dead dogs lie?"

I was stunned. "Dad, you don't understand! I'm trying to tell you I forgive you and I love you for the first time in my life—and it's because of Jesus. He's given me a love for you that I could never have without him."

Nothing I said mattered. Dad refused my forgiveness. Mom didn't verbally accept my forgiveness that night, but she did try to calm my dad and make him listen to what I had to say. Her actions spoke as loud as any words of acceptance could have.

A couple years later, I flew to Dad's bedside in a nursing home where he lay dying of cancer. Each day, for a week, I told him

Kitty Chappell

about the death and resurrection of Jesus Christ. During my last visit, I said, "Dad, you know I could never have loved and forgiven you if Jesus hadn't changed my heart." He just stared at me dismally. With my heart heavy with urgency, I persisted. "Dad, the only way you can go to heaven is to believe that Jesus paid for your sins. You must seek God's forgiveness before you die."

When Dad finally spoke, his words astonished me. "What I did was so evil, I can't even speak it."

"You're right," I agreed. "What you did was very evil. But you don't have to speak it because God knows what you did. All you have to do is ask him to forgive you of your sins."

Dad remained silent. I pointed my index finger upward as I spoke the last words I ever said to my dad, "In heaven, okay?"

A good friend called three days after my dad died. She'd visited him the night before his death and assured me he had, indeed, done what I'd asked him to do. My heart soared! *I will see Dad in heaven—where there are no webs.*

ꙭ

Several years following her father's death, Lynne reconciled with her mother who also accepted Christ on her deathbed. Lynne and Steve, married over thirty years, spent six years traveling by motorhome throughout the United States, volunteering their labor with MMAP (Mobile Missionary Assistance Program). Steve then returned to full-time work with Raytheon as a network hardware engineer with the U-2 program at Beale Air Force Base in Marysville, California, during which time he spent a few months each year working in The United Arab Emirates, Korea, or Germany. As a speaker for Stonecroft Ministries, Lynne shares her story nationwide and speaks at women's retreats as well. She is author of a workbook, *Unbridled Surrender–God's Answer to Overcoming*, which includes her story. Lynne uses her workbook in Bible study sessions to help others overcome similar backgrounds. For ordering information, contact Lynne at: L.s.bennett@syix.com.

> But when you are praying, first forgive anyone you are holding a grudge against, so that your Father in heaven will forgive your sins, too.
>
> Mark 11:25

> We are most like beasts when we kill. We are most like men when we judge. We are most like God when we forgive.
>
> —Author unknown

> To err is human, to forgive divine.
>
> —Alexander Pope

> The weak can never forgive. Forgiveness is the attribute of the strong.
>
> Mahatma Gandhi

> Forgiveness is not an emotion…Forgiveness is an act of the will, and the will can function regardless of the temperature of the heart.
>
> —Corrie ten Boom

WE MUST FORGIVE OURSELVES

Maybe you have no trouble forgiving others but you can't forgive yourself. Somehow you feel to blame for all the pain you've experienced, or you feel shame that you couldn't do more to change the circumstances. You wonder if you invited the tragedies that occurred. You let the perpetrator place his guilt upon you and you still carry the heavy shame upon your back. Maybe you *have* committed some terrible sins. (Many of us have.) They hang around your neck like an albatross, and you berate yourself daily. The origin of your feelings of guilt and shame isn't important. The point is you don't have to continue carrying them. Ask God to forgive you and he will. And when he does, it's a done deal. You have no right to insult his forgiveness and love by continuing to hate yourself or to keep asking him over and over to do what he's already done. He may wonder about your hearing or your short term memory for this is what he said about your sins. "I—yes, I alone—will blot out your sins for my own sake and will never think of them again" (Isaiah 43:25).

We feel helpless when old feelings of guilt pop up. Our regenerated heart is very sensitive for it's not part of our new nature to *want* to sin. Therefore, when we are reminded of specific past sins we can become overwhelmed again with feelings of guilt because we know we committed them. Caught up in our feelings, we forget the facts. God pardoned those sins! But what can we do to stop the repeated onslaught of guilt feelings?

I had just concluded my speech at a Celebrate Recovery meeting when a huge recently paroled ex-felon lumbered toward me. I tried to ignore his countless tattoos and body piercings.

Without introducing himself, and with a firm set to his unshaven jaw, he jumped right in with what worried him.

"When you spoke about forgiveness you said we must also forgive ourselves. But you don't understand. I've done some terrible things, how could I *ever* forgive myself?"

Smiling with understanding, I answered, "More importantly, has God forgiven you?"

"Yes."

"But are you sure?" I countered, wanting his full attention.

"Absolutely, without a doubt!"

Looking steadily into his eyes, I asked slowly, "Do you think you are greater than God?"

Shocked, he replied, "Of course not, no one is greater than God!"

"Then why do you think your sins are so great that not even God, Creator of the universe, the King of kings, and Lord of lords can forget them? Don't you think that's arrogant?"

He blinked and with furrowed brows admitted, "I never thought of it that way. But why do I still feel guilty?"

"Think about it. Who do you think is reminding you of those past sins? It isn't God. It's his enemy, Satan. He knows you have been set free once and for all by God, but he wants to keep you in bondage, bound to him in your mind through your past sins." He listened intently as I spoke. "Do you want to know what helps me?"

After his nod, I continued. "I say, 'Thank you, Satan, for reminding me of those old sins, I'd almost forgotten about them! This reminds me to thank and praise my heavenly Father again for his total forgiveness of those awful sins. Isn't he wonderful for doing that?' And then I start thanking God. Satan absolutely hates to hear God praised, so he leaves. He's not stupid, so he rarely comes around to remind me anymore— he knows what will happen. Does that make sense?" I asked.

"It sure does!" he answered with a big grin. "Thanks," he said, pumping my hand vigorously and walking away with head held high and steps much lighter.

Your steps will also be lighter when you refuse to carry those old sins that Satan wants to pile on your back.

STEP TWO:
ACCOUNTABILITY

We must assume responsibility for our thoughts and actions. How can we obey God if we don't take control of our thoughts? This is the most difficult of all battles! It is an ongoing, lifetime commitment that requires studying (not just reading) the Bible and praying for understanding—and then putting God's principles into practice.

When I first began to understand the importance of assuming responsibility for my thoughts and actions, I was struck by a quote I read that described me perfectly:

> Men are disturbed, not by the things that happen, but by their opinion of the things that happen.
>
> —Epictetus, ancient philosopher

So impressed was I with this statement that I typed copies of it and taped them to the mirrors in my bathrooms as reminders to not react to everything but to seek the truth in every situation. These typed nuggets of wisdom were immensely helpful as I strived to develop the habit of not reacting by jumping to unfounded conclusions with little or no fact. However, due to my negative past it required persistent determination—and sometimes an uncomfortable object lesson. The following is an example of how my mind continued to go into negative automatic drive when I lost control.

As I walked down our local street one day, a member of my church walked toward me. I smiled and slowed my pace, ready for a brief chat. But she didn't even break stride, didn't return my smile, and passed me without a word.

Of all the nerve—she snubbed me! Why? I've done nothing to her. My mind worked overtime trying to uncover the reason I was snubbed. *It must be because I disagreed with her at the committee meeting last week. Well, give me a break! My opinion is just as good as hers—even though I'm not an attorney's wife!* I fumed and worried about it for the rest of the week.

The following Sunday, I sat several pews behind her at church. *How can she sit there looking pious after treating me so rudely? What a hypocrite! And I always thought she was such a great Christian! Just goes to show how you never really know about someone.*

Following the service I was engaged in conversation with a friend when I felt a touch on my shoulder. It was the attorney's wife. "Kitty, I want to apologize for not acknowledging you the other day. I was so deep in thought that I didn't even realize it was you until you had passed by. I'm sorry. I hope you didn't think I deliberately ignored you, for I would never do that."

"Oh...thank you," I stammered in surprise. "No, I didn't give it a second thought," I lied.

I recalled the quote on my mirror. What a perfect example of blowing something out of proportion with my opinion. I was wrong on every count! That incident motivated me to control my thoughts and become more objective and less subjective.

But how could I do that when I wasn't even sure what those words meant? I thought that being objective meant I was against something. Mr. Webster taught me the difference.

Objective: expressing or involving the use of facts without distortion by personal feelings, prejudices, or interpretations.

Example: Every person is born a unique individual with value and potential, despite race or environment, and that includes me. (This is fact, based not only upon the Bible, but the consensus of rational mankind.)

Subjective: knowledge as conditioned by personal mental characteristics or states; modified or affected by personal views, experience, or background.

Example: Because I was born into a bad environment, I don't have a chance. I am inferior and don't deserve anything better than my beginning environment. (This view is based upon feelings and totally lacking in fact.)

There are three elements to objectivity: the acceptance of truth, the pursuit of truth, and the adjustment to truth.

Examples:

Acceptance of Truth

I was created by God as a unique person of immense value. I accept the truth that among the trillions of individuals already born, and who will be born, there is only one me. God loves me, and I have something to contribute to this world.

Pursuit of Truth

No matter how uncomfortable I may be with the truth, I will strive to seek it and to live by it. I will attempt to be honest with myself at all times, for only then can I be honest with others.

Adjustment to Truth

I will adjust to the truth by assuming responsibility for my thoughts and actions. I will break the habit of making excuses and blaming others or circumstances for my failures and mistakes. I will do my best to rectify my wrongs and apologize for the mistakes I make—regardless of the cost. I will not curse myself for my errors, but I will learn from them and become stronger.

We must become lovers and seekers of truth. Seeing the truth, however, can be painful, for it always calls for action. That is why we so often try to avoid it.

We try to escape from truth by hiding from it.

We eat ourselves into obesity but are still hungry.

We drink and drug ourselves into emotional and mental derelicts and remain thirsty.

We try to outrun truth by busying ourselves. We go from one person, party, or activity to another until we are exhausted. We fear that in the vulnerability of being alone, honesty will seduce us, and we will be faced with the reality of what we don't want to see.

We plunge into our career, our work, our hobbies, and become overachievers. We seek to build with our hands an image worth viewing, but we never succeed.

We work feverishly behind the walls of religion, observing mindless rituals, counting prayers, and stockpiling good works in hopes that the "naughty and nice" scale will tip in our favor. When will we realize that heaven is not a reward but a gift? No matter what we do, truth is still there, waiting to be acknowledged.

> Truth is incontrovertible. Panic may resent it; ignorance may deride it; malice may distort it; but there it is.
>
> Winston Churchill

MOI? SELF-CENTERED?

I recall reading an article, when I was in my thirties, written by a psychiatrist who stated that overly sensitive people are self-centered. He explained that when such individuals are chronically offended, it is because their world centers on *them*, what happens to *them*, and *their* feelings. He challenged his readers to take note of how many times *I*, *me*, and *my* are used in conversations (this included self-talk).

I recall I was initially offended by the psychiatrist's statement. *Me? Self-centered? I'm one of the most unselfish people I know. I'm always doing things for others!*

As I struggled honestly with his statements, however, I realized that I *was* self-centered. I had a chronic case of *I* trouble. In almost every situation, *I* was the center of my concern. *I* was hurt, *I* was treated unfairly, *I* was misunderstood, *I* disagreed, *I* would never have said or done that, and *I* would have done it differently...*I, I, I.* My entire thought world system revolved around me.

It became apparent that I needed to think less about me and my feelings and more about others—where *they* were coming from and what *they* were feeling. When I started being honest with myself, I had to admit that most of the "unselfish" things I did for others were actually selfish. Yes, I wanted to help them, but my primary joy came from feeling good about myself. I wanted and needed the praise of others. And the best way to get it was to always be doing something for others, even if it meant sacrificing precious time with my husband and children. That way I could say to myself, *See what a good person I am!*

Through my pursuit of honesty, I asked God to help me develop a genuine love and concern for others. Guess what? My self-centeredness lessened, and I began to develop a proper self-esteem. We hear and read much about the need for a positive self-image, but what we need is a proper self-image. When we do wrong, we should feel bad! Our guilt can be used as a tool to get us back on the right track. As our proper self-image develops, we will develop more confidence to scrutinize ourselves honestly.

Once I discovered that I wouldn't crumble from my own scrutiny, I was freed from the need to appear perfect. I relaxed and became more open and transparent with others without fear that my flaws might be seen. I discovered that when I accepted myself, others accepted me. They related more to my humanness than to my prior facade of "perfection." My credibility grew—not only with others but with myself.

Of all that is involved in the development of good character and a strong, healthy self-esteem, I believe the most important is a sincere desire to please God. This desire leads one to the foot of God's throne and to obedience. Only when we walk with God in obedience can we taste the fruit of his promises.

> The promises of God are of no value to us until, through obedience, we come to understand the nature of God. We may read some things in the Bible every day for a year and they may mean nothing to us. Then, because we have been obedient to God in some small detail, we suddenly see what God means and his nature is instantly opened up to us.
>
> Oswald Chambers, *My Utmost for His Highest*
>
> Our goal is to please him.
>
> 2 Corinthians 5:9

WHAT IF?

Just as self-centered thoughts do not please God, neither do anxious and fearful thoughts.

When our children were small, I sometimes accompanied my husband on business trips. I wanted to go and was a great help to him, but I suffered anxiety over leaving the children.

What if they get sick? What if they have an accident? What if the house catches on fire? I conjured up all kinds of horrible things that could happen while I wasn't there. It didn't matter that we had competent, mature babysitters, a telephone on the premises, and lived near a hospital. I worried anyway.

CHANGING THE "WHAT IF" PROGRAMS

Then something happened that gave me power to go in the opposite direction. After overdoing it with yard work one day, I found myself in my chiropractor's office. Because I had not gone in promptly for an adjustment, that area in my back was particularly tender. The chiropractor positioned me for manipulation and instructed me to relax. Because that area was so painful, I feared the adjustment might hurt, and I couldn't relax.

After a couple of unsuccessful attempts, he said, "Wiggle the toes on your right foot." When I wiggled my toes, he made the adjustment—without pain.

"Why did I have to wiggle my toes?" I asked.

"When you concentrated on wiggling your toes," he explained, "your focus shifted from your pain to your toes. You relaxed, and I could make the adjustment."

Driving home, I thought, *Why wouldn't the "wiggle your toes" principle work in other areas?*

I had read or heard somewhere that worry is merely negative imagination. Could I break the chain of worry by substituting positive imagination for the negative? When we left on our next trip and the old negative thought patterns began to play, I changed tactics. I substituted positive "what ifs" for the usual negatives.

What if, while we are gone, the babysitter is watching the children playing in the front yard and a kind white-haired gentleman walks by and stops to chat with them? He is a lonely widower with no children or grandchildren of his own. Our kids really take to him. The babysitter carefully observes him and decides he's just a harmless, kind, lonely old man who loves children. He chats with them for a while and then resumes his walk.

I build this scenario to the point that when we return home, we become friends with the kind old man and adopt him into our family circle. Several years later, he dies and leaves a fortune to our children. (And we had thought he was penniless!) Our children's college education was secured. Our son became a surgeon and our daughter an attorney.

Wait a minute, my logical mind interjects. *This is a stupid story! Just because you are gone on a business trip, you think that's going to happen? Not likely!* But I, now knowing that I have the power to wiggle my mental toes and break the negative focus, reply, *That's true. But neither is it likely that my house is going to burn down just because I am gone.*

After our second trip, I was free of the negative worries—forever. I received more than a manipulation that freed me from physical pain that day at the chiropractor's office. I discovered a method of attitude adjustment that freed me from a lifetime of mental and emotional pain.

STEP THREE:
GRATITUDE

Thus far we have covered two of the three steps necessary to become an overcomer—forgiveness (with its three facets) and responsibility for our thoughts and actions. Gratitude is the third step. Omit it, and we cannot complete our journey. Gratitude protects us from following the tempting siren call of self-pity into the quagmire of quicksand. And without gratitude we can never know joy.

> Gratitude is not only the greatest of virtues, but the parent of all the others.
>
> —Cicero

> Gratitude is the fairest blossom which springs from the soul.
>
> —Henry Ward Beecher

THE KEY TO GRATITUDE

"But how can I be grateful when I have so many problems?" you ask. "And who doesn't want to feel grateful all the time? It's hard when worries press in upon me from every side, and I feel like the only light at the end of the tunnel really is the proverbial freight train. Believe me, I would love to enter into that elusive state of gratitude, but sometimes the door is shut tight. What do I do then?"

Trust. "Trust in the Lord with all your heart; do not depend on your own understanding" (Proverbs 3:5). Trust is the golden key that unlocks the door of gratitude. But can we really lean completely on God and trust Him? We've already seen that we can't put any weight on our own understanding—we believe a lie too easily. We believe the lies we tell ourselves and the lies that others tell us.

On an earthly level, we want to trust people, but first we need to know that they are trustworthy. How many people do you trust completely—people to whom you would entrust all of your earthly possessions, even your very life? You are fortunate if you can name more than two or three people.

Why do you trust them? Because they have integrity—and they have a good track record. They have kept every promise they made to you. Or at least they have tried.

God is that kind of friend. There are many powerful descriptions of God in Scripture—good, wise, loving, patient, just, righteous, perfect, holy. There is another description, however, that you may not have considered.

> This truth gives them confidence that they have eternal life, which God—who does not lie—promised them before the world began.
>
> Titus 1:2

Why can't God lie? I asked myself after first reading that verse. *He can do anything he wants—he's God!*

Later, I contemplated Isaiah 43:25: "I—yes, I alone—will blot out your sins for my own sake and will never think of them again." I marveled at a love so strong that it could not only forgive a person of his or her sins but also never bring them up again! I had been forgiven by friends for wrongs I had done, but sometimes they reminded me of my past offenses—to either humiliate me or to make me feel obligated.

Why would God make and keep such a promise? Four little words, tucked away in the middle of that verse, answer this question: "for my own sake."

What a strange phrase! I thought, *I wonder what it means?* Later that day, I overheard a conversation between two men discussing a mutual friend. "One thing I appreciate about Jim is his integrity. When he says he'll do something, I don't ever have to worry about it—it's as good as done. He always keeps his word."

That's it! I thought, recalling the phrase in Isaiah, "for my own sake." *God will keep every promise he makes—not because of who we are, but because of who he is. And that is why God cannot lie.*

God doesn't have integrity—God is integrity. He is the author of truth. When he makes a promise, it's as good as done. His consistency, based on who he is, will never be affected by our moods, our circumstances, or our actions. God is a holy and just God who will always keep his word. And for that assurance, our every breath should be one of undying gratitude.

HOW TO BECOME
MORE GRATEFUL

We set the stage for misery when we ignore our blessings. Show me a person who is consistently unhappy, and I'll show you a person who is consistently ungrateful.

Tip #1: Don't compare yourself or your circumstances with others.

The person who plays the comparison game will never be happy. There will always be someone around who is smarter, better looking, richer, and more talented. Many survivors are plagued by an inferiority complex, which will surface in one of two ways. They either have a competitive need to outdo every one around them to prove their own value, or they undervalue themselves and insist that the talents they possess are inferior. Both attitudes are incorrect. For many years, I suffered from inferiority feelings that match those of the second type—and sometimes I still struggle.

Both perceptions can be corrected when we focus on the truth about our value. Our worth lies not in what we do but in who we are. We are beloved children of God—daughters and sons of the King. There is no greater rank. We have "already arrived." We can't do one thing to motivate our heavenly Father to love us any more than he already does. When we accept this truth, we won't feel the need to prove our worth to God or anyone else—especially ourselves.

Sometimes we are dissatisfied because others seem to have more and better possessions. We would be content if only we had a bigger house, nicer clothes, a fancier car, smarter children, a more thoughtful husband—then we would be happy. But how do we know when enough is enough? Regardless of how much you have, you can still be grateful—grateful that you have life, that God loves you, grateful for the specific things God has already given you, grateful in all circumstances!

I have learned how to be content with whatever I have.

Philippians 4:11

Since we have a choice as to whether we will be content or discontented, doesn't it make sense to choose the attitude that will create joy? Discontentment only leads to more pain—such as envy and greed. Did you know that we are never more like Satan than when we envy? It was because of envy that Satan rebelled against God.

Besides, things may not always be as they appear. The woman you may at this moment be envying may have her own secret desires to live your life. A statement printed at the top of a note

I received from a friend one day says it well: "The grass that appears greener on the other side may be only Astroturf."

Conclusion: *If we don't compare ourselves with others we are able to be grateful.*

Tip #2: Reprogram your attitude.

The only real handicap in life is a bad attitude. Remember how I retrained my mental muscles to reject critical thoughts of my husband? Remember how when a critical, faultfinding thought popped into my mind, I deliberately looked for ten positive attributes in my husband? The same exercise routine can be used to build gratitude. Stop complaining, and strengthen your gratitude muscles. For each complaint your mind focuses upon, wiggle your mental toes and look for ten blessings. This should be easy since we have countless more blessings than disadvantages. Then thank God for each blessing.

Conclusion: *If we look for blessings, we will be too busy to complain.*

Tip #3: Choose the proper residence for your mind.

"Fix your thoughts on what is true, and honorable, and right, and pure, and lovely, and admirable. Think about things that are excellent and worthy of praise" (Philippians 4:8). How could the apostle Paul, as he sat in a dungeon, tell us to be thankful regardless of our circumstances? Because he knew from experience that when we give thanks in every situation, every situation becomes bearable. Besides, his body may have been in a dungeon, but his mind didn't dwell there.

If you decided to build a new home and you could build it any place you wanted, would you build it in the middle of the city dump? Then why would you allow the most beautiful possession you own to reside there? Since the mind is a terrible thing to waste, doesn't it deserve to dwell in a healthy and beautiful residence instead of a wasteland? If you are currently dwelling in the dumps, move. It's a stinky, miserable place that results in "stinkin' thinkin'"—a mind-set that you and your family and friends should not be expected to endure. Move your mind to a brighter place that focuses on good things, not the bad, and practice gratitude. For without gratitude, your life will remain miserable even though you move into a mansion.

Conclusion: *If you want to develop an attitude of gratitude, then house your mind in pleasant thoughts.*

Tip #4: Learn to "be thankful in all circumstances" (1 Thessalonians 5:18).

I recall an incident that occurred right after I first set out to develop an attitude of gratitude. I was running behind schedule one morning, as usual. After loading my car with what I needed for a day of busy activities, I slammed the car door shut, started the engine, and was backing out of the garage when it happened—the zipper in my slacks broke.

A month earlier, I would have come unglued. "Oh, great! This is going to be a lousy day!" I would have fumed and fretted, wasting valuable energy that was needed for a busy day.

However, I was determined to live out Paul's admonition to "give thanks in every situation." I stopped the engine, took a deep breath, and thought, *There's got to be something in this situation for which to give thanks. I looked for reasons to be thankful,* and guess what? I found them.

As I dashed inside to change, I whispered, "Thank you, Lord, that I picked up my other dressy pair of slacks from the cleaners yesterday. And thank you that my zipper broke at this moment instead of later this morning. And thank you that it was my zipper that broke and not my ankle."

It took only a few minutes to change and I was back on the road. The most important change I made that morning, however, was not my change of clothes, but my change in attitude. I changed a grumpy attitude into a grateful one. It was my choice.

Conclusion: *We don't have to let unwanted circumstances control our behavior. We can find blessings in every situation.*

If you work each day on the above steps, before you know it, your complaints will cease, and you will enjoy life as a grateful person.

JOY — A CHOSEN FRUIT

My friend, Dr. Curt Brannan, related an incident that occurred during one of his visits to a local rest home when he was our pastor in Ojai, California. One of the inhabitants there, named Charlie, was a delightful man who was confined to a wheelchair. As he zipped around the facility, Charlie was always happy, spreading sunshine wherever he went. Curt knew he experienced persistent pain and marveled at Charlie's consistent thoughtfulness and cheery attitude.

One day Curt asked him, "Charlie, why are you so cheerful and happy all of the time?"

Charlie grinned and answered, "Because that's the way I want to be."

> I've noticed that people are generally about as happy as they make up their minds to be.
>
> —Abraham Lincoln

> A cheerful heart is good medicine, but a broken spirit saps a person's strength.
>
> Proverbs 17:22

Peter Haile writes in his book *The Difference God Makes—Living as if God Matters*:

> If we have been born again, we have been born of God's
> Spirit; we have been infused with his very life; we have
> been made partners of the divine nature; we are God's
> heirs, God's offspring. It is now our nature to want to do
> what God wants us to do. This was brought home to me
> once by a friend who said, "When I'm tempted, I stop to
> remember that a Christian can do whatever he wants to
> do."
>
> I replied, "Now wait a minute. I thought that's just what a
> Christian couldn't do."
>
> And then he said to me, "Do you want to be unloving? Do
> you want to be selfish? Do you want to be impure?"
>
> Immediately I knew that what he had said was true. I did
> not want to be selfish; in fact, it was the last thing I wanted
> to be.

As ransomed children of the King, the purest desire of our heart is to walk closely with Christ and bear evidence that with his help we can do anything we want! We want to love, not hate, forgive, not resent, and trust, not fear. And we can do all these things. Christ paid for our freedom and we can overcome anything! Such good news bears repeating, Christ paid for our freedom! We are free! Talk about joy!

"If that don't light your fire," says my friend Beth Christensen, "then your wood's wet!"

THE PROOF OF THE PUDDING
IS IN THE EATING

Are these just empty words written in a book by a writer because they fit in with the subject of overcoming versus merely surviving? Is the author really an overcomer?

You decide.

- I no longer suffer from nightmares about my father.

- I watch court scenes on television and participate as an objective juror without reliving the old negative feelings of anger and shame I felt during Dad's trial.

- While I am satisfied that my father served time in prison for his crime against my mother, I feel compassion when I think of him and his wasted life.

- My father was wrong in all that he did that caused my family and me pain, but I forgave him. I haven't the slightest residue of anger toward him. I am free of resentment and bitterness.

- I speak of my father, not with disdain or a rise in blood pressure, but in a respectful, calm, and sad manner.

- I do not blame my father for my shortcomings, my weaknesses, or my failures. I assume full responsibility for all of my choices in life.

- I refuse to entertain thoughts of self-pity, regardless of what happens in life. I have obliterated "Why me?" from my mental vocabulary. Instead, I ask, "Why not me? God's grace is sufficient to help me in any situation." I have changed my "why?" to "how?" "How, Lord, can You be honored in this situation?"

Nothing robs one's strength and vitality so much as self-absorption. There is no greater waste of time than self-pity, preoccupation with self; it fragments and dissipates that which you want to be about.

—Tim Hansel, *You Gotta Keep Dancin'*

Photographs of my father holding us children when we were little, as well as photos of his second family, are included on our family photo wall. Are they there because he is a great example of fatherhood? No. They are there because he is my father. They are there to serve as evidence that each of Dad's children—my brother, my sister, and I—have forgiven him.

When a friend of mine mentioned to someone that my father's pictures are on our photo wall, the other person's response was, "That's sick!"

But is it? Including my father's photos on our wall evidences another truth. Not only do I hold no resentment toward him, neither am I burdened with feelings of shame. I don't live in fear that someone might find out about the wrong choices my father made. Truth is the key that unlocks the door to shame. I use this key as an opportunity to show that, with God's help, our right choices can overcome the harm done by the wrong choices of others. It is also an opportunity to point out the importance of our making the right choices, since they always affect those around us. So am I sick, or am I healthy?

I thank God for what he has helped me to become through my negative experiences. Of course, I am not thankful *for* my father's abuse. *That* would be sick! But I am thankful that the evil committed by my father is being overcome by the good that God is able to accomplish in the lives of my siblings and myself.

I thank God for all blessings—not just on Thanksgiving Day, but every day. Because, like Charlie in the rest home, "That's the way I want to be!" Always grateful—and joyful.

JOY IN HARD TIMES

A bird doesn't sing because he has an answer—he sings
because he has a song.

—Joan Anglund

Choosing joy will provide new strength and vigor, not only
for today but also for the future—when the rough times come.
And they will. We would be wise to get mentally prepared, as
did Habakkuk.

> Even though the fig trees have no blossoms, and there are
> no grapes on the vines; even though the olive crop fails,
> and the fields lie empty and barren; even though the flocks
> die in the fields, and the cattle barns are empty, yet I will
> rejoice in the LORD! I will be joyful in the God of my
> salvation!
>
> Habakkuk 3:17-18

Why does Habakkuk determine to rejoice in such dire circumstances should they come? Because, regardless of our shifting
sands of circumstance, no matter how difficult the winding, stony
and slippery uphill path, nor how dizzying the heights of our
obstacles, God is our constant source of strength. "The Sovereign
LORD is my strength! He makes me as surefooted as a deer, able
to tread upon the heights" (Habakkuk 3:19). Habakkuk knows
that God will lead him to higher pastures of hope and provide

him stability that will help him to dig his heels in and avoid sliding into the bleak valley of despondency below.

When the California recession drove Jerry and me from our beautiful home in Oakhurst, California, it completely changed the direction of our lives. We had struggled for several years to make payments on our two-acre parcel in the mountains near the beautiful Yosemite National Park and had designed and built what we thought would be our retirement home. We had walked through the wooded terrain, laying the lines for our dream home to catch the perfect view of the valley below and the snow-covered mountains beyond that would be highlighted by the late afternoon sun. Before we even broke ground, I planted daffodil bulbs on each side of the deer path that led downhill through the gnarled manzanita trees, oaks, and pines to the seasonal creek and waterfall below. When finished and furnished, our home was even more beautiful than we had hoped. But the recession was worsening.

One by one, we saw businesses flee California and relocate their businesses to other states. One close friend urged us to do the same. "Don't wait until it's too late," he warned. Some had already waited too long and had lost everything, including their home. But we refused to acknowledge the density of the dark clouds on the economy's horizon.

"California is our home—how can we leave it?" we asked each other. "Besides, California has weathered recessions before—it will turn around soon."

But it didn't. We ran out of money before the recession ran out of breath. We not only lost our business but every penny we had saved and invested for our retirement. And we were deep in debt.

But I prepared myself to let go. Even as I dug and developed sixteen beds for my favorite roses, lovingly transported from the Ojai Valley where we had previously lived, I recall thinking, *I may not get to enjoy this rose garden very long—but someone will.* I reminded myself often of something Corrie ten Boom had written about not hanging onto things in life too tightly because it hurt too much when God had to pry her fingers loose.

Three-and-a-half years after moving into our home, we closed its doors and sadly turned over the keys to a property management firm to lease, since we had been unable to sell it. We were moving to the deserts of Arizona. At an age when we had hoped to be in a position to retire, we had to start all over again in a strange land, broke and heavyhearted. But before we left, I again prepared myself. As I stood looking out over the valley from our bay window in the breakfast nook off our country kitchen, I made a decision.

When I am living in the middle of the desert—a place I always said I would never live—and I am in my tiny apartment kitchen with no windows, I will not long for the beauty of this oak-framed garden window above my sink where I watch the deer walk to the creek below nor the openness of this nook that allows the awesomeness of nature to filter through its glass walls. Nor will I covet the storage space in these wall-to-wall solid oak cabinets. I will not complain, nor will I make myself miserable by comparing what I don't have with what I once had. I will thank God for this short chapter of life and its beautiful memories. I will thank him daily for that little apartment, the brevity of the time it will take to clean it, and for all of my blessings, beginning with my loving, hardworking husband and the good health that enables us to again labor fulltime in the workforce—at sixty years of age. I will trust my present and future circumstances to my Lord, who has never failed me.

And that's exactly what happened.

Wise men never sit and wail their loss, but cheerily seek how to redress their harms.

—William Shakespeare

I believe my past losses taught me to let go quickly. Because I had to leave my home and everything dear to me at the age of nineteen, I was better prepared for future losses. Through experience, I learned that things are temporary but God's love is permanent.

It was hard for Jerry to step over the ashes of our California business, leave the mountain home that he had worked so hard on to the care of tenants because we could not sell it, and submit to a new economic harness by working for strangers in the desert of Arizona. Those first several years were difficult. We rarely saw each other. I worked at night at a local hospital, and he worked during the day as an estimator for a commercial glass company.

But God did not abandon us in the desert. With the help of a young partner, Jerry started another commercial glass business which flourished and steadily grew. I was able to take early retirement and pursue my writing and speaking. After paying off old debts, we bought a two-story lakefront home. Jerry found a used eighteen-foot pontoon boat, and we began to relax again as we enjoyed romantic moonlit nights cruising around the lake. We thanked God for our blessings as we watched the ducks swim lazily in our cove. But we never took the beauty for granted, nor did we sink our roots into its soil. We knew it was temporary. We understood that whether we left our new haven by choice one day or if we were forced to leave and live out our lives in a cozy shack due to another unexpected financial reversal, we were not going to worry about it—we trusted our Lord. We had already learned that far more important than the kind of house one lives in is the kind of attitude that lives within the house.

It is imperative that each of us prepares for the hard times ahead. We need to think about what we are unwilling to give up. Is it our independence, our status, our health, home, child, or mate? It is our nature to want to dig our heels in and, with arms crossed like a stubborn child, cry, "No, Lord! Don't let this happen! I could not handle it!" But our fingers will bleed when they are pried loose from that which we are unwilling to release, and a rip will appear in our heart through which our joy will escape.

In 1988, I was diagnosed with endometrial cancer and faced immediate surgery. The doctors believed the cancer had spread into the lymph glands and were certain I would require additional treatment. I was at peace, but Jerry was devastated. "God has to let you survive. He knows I can't live without you!" he said the night before my surgery, eyes tearing.

"The Lord doesn't know any such thing!" I said gently. "You don't live for Kitty Chappell—you live for God! You can live without me, but you can't live without him. You must let me go whether or not I survive."

The next morning when I arose, he had been up for hours, praying. His eyes glowed as he took my hands and said, "I did it—I let you go! I will trust the Lord whatever happens, for I know he will be with me." I faced my surgery that morning free of concern, for Jerry and I as a team had placed ourselves in God's hands. The cancer was intact and surgery removed it all.

I believe Jerry's ability to face and accept my mortality helped prepare him for the day when he had to accept his own. In October of 2000, Jerry was diagnosed with cancer—non-Hodgkin lymphoma. He told me the news hit him hard. For over an hour, he said he just drove around, wondering how he was going to tell me, and asking God, "Why me, Lord?" By the time he arrived home, however, he had accepted it.

He underwent a series of successful radiation treatments in good spirits. He did well for three years, returning only for routine blood work, scans, and checkups. But in 2003, the cancer returned with a vengeance. In six months, between scans, a huge tumor developed near his apex—too close to his heart to operate. Jerry underwent several rounds of chemotherapy, but never missed a day at the office. He'd rise early, drive to Scottsdale, where he underwent his infusions, eat a restaurant breakfast, and then drive straight to his office in Chandler, where he worked the rest of the day.

The tumor shrank somewhat, but not enough. He patiently endured another round of chemo. Through it all, his spirit was dauntless. His smile and sense of humor lit up the offices where he went for treatment, scans, and workups.

One day someone asked, "How can you be so cheerful through all of this?"

"Because I'm in a win-win situation—either all of this treatment will cure me, or I'll go home to heaven where I won't need it." He grinned and then added, "I can't lose for winning."

Yes, Jerry was going through hard times—but he never lost his joy.

> Don't be dejected and sad, for the joy of the LORD is your strength.
>
> Nehemiah 8:10

When we accept the bottom line, we can live on the top—where joy dwells. When we trust our future to God, think of and accept the absolute worst that can happen, what is there left to fear?

> Fear knocked at the door.
>
> Faith answered.
>
> And lo, no one was there.
>
> –Author unknown.

As we walk through life, reality teaches us that everything we have, regardless of our precautions, can be taken from us.

Stocks crash, banks fail, economies collapse, investments turn sour—tornadoes, cyclones, fires, and floods can destroy our home and everything in it. Even our loved ones can be taken from us through a plane crash, an automobile accident, a sniper's bullet, or a terminal disease.

Jerry and I knew that all too well. He lost his father, three brothers, a sister, and a brother-in-law to cancer. I lost my maternal grandfather and two step-grandfathers to cancer. I knew I could also lose my Jerry—and that would break my heart. But I also believed that should that happen, my joy in the Lord would remain intact. I would hurt, yes, but life would not be over for me no matter how much I missed Jerry. God would be there again to take my heart and mend it with his loving hands—just as he had always done.

So far as God is concerned, if we belong to him, we can overcome all of these things—with his help. In fact, he expects us to overcome because of who we are. And we should expect it!

> But you belong to God, my dear children. You have already won a victory...because the Spirit who lives in you is greater than the spirit who lives in the world.
>
> 1 John 4:4

> No, despite all these things, overwhelming victory is ours through Christ, who loved us. And I am convinced that nothing can ever separate us from God's love. Neither death nor life, neither angels nor demons, neither our fears for today nor our worries about tomorrow—not even the powers of hell can separate us from God's love.
>
> Romans 8:37-39

Jerry planned to retire in December of 2005 and build a single-story home he had just designed, but the cancer suddenly spread to his lungs. Following a two-week hospitalization and a valiant short battle, my sweet Jerry went home to be with the Lord in May of that year. Though my belief and trust in God were intact, my feelings weren't. The gaping wound left in my heart when Jerry was ripped from it felt as though it would never heal. The poem below, which I had written years earlier, best expresses those feelings.

WHEN I HURT, LORD

When I hurt, Lord, and fear my pain will slay me
As I fight my unwanted flood of circumstances;
When life's stormy waters would pull me under
As they lash relentlessly at my very foundation,
Lift me up, Lord.
When the strongest hope I have is to but awaken
From a bad dream and see life as I'd like it to be,
But cries from my soul shout the pain of reality
In my ears, and my eyes see things as they are,
Help me trust, Lord.
When my soul is hollow with hurt and I feel fragile
And wonder why, when yesterday I felt so strong;
When I fear I will shatter into a million pieces
Unless you embrace me with your arms of love,
Hold me together, Lord,
Until I am mended.

–Kitty Chappell

Do not be afraid, for I have ransomed you. I have called you by name; you are mine. When you go through deep waters and great trouble, I will be with you. When you go through rivers of difficulty, you will not drown! For I am the LORD, your God...your Savior...you are precious to me. You are honored, and I love you.

Isaiah 43:1-4

God never meant for the pain in our heart to be more than temporary. His word validates that truth.

And now, dear brothers and sisters, we want you to know what will happen to the believers who have died so you will not grieve like people who have no hope. For since we believe that Jesus died and was raised to life again, we also believe that when Jesus returns, God will bring back with him the believers who have died.

1 Thessalonians 4:13-14

It has been over seven years now, and my heart is whole again—healed by God just as I had believed. From the moment God welcomed Jerry with open arms into heaven, he embraced me with his love and wisdom. I learned quickly that when I focused on where Jerry is and not on where he isn't, my pain subsided. Shifting the focus from my pain to Jerry's joy helped me avoid self-pity, which would have prolonged my pain and hindered the healing process. The old saying, "If you truly love someone, you will want what is best for them, even if it's not what you want," helped me with this focus. How many times have I looked up to heaven and whispered through tears, "Honey, I am so happy for you—you have truly 'escaped the tempter's snare.'"

Yes, we can overcome the deepest heartaches—and with our joy intact.

You will live in joy and peace. The mountains and hills will burst into song, and the trees of the field will clap their hands.

Isaiah 55:12

Soaring above the Ashes on the Wings of Forgiveness 253

Once again God proved in my life there can be joy in the hard times. We will never be robbed of that joy, no matter how hard the circumstances, if we choose to live our lives for God and not for ourselves. We can choose joy or self-pity, forgiveness or bitterness, life or death—but only we can make those choices.

> Today I have given you the choice between life and death, between blessings and curses. Now I call on heaven and earth to witness the choice you make. Oh, that you would choose life, so that you and your descendants might live! You can make this choice by loving the LORD your God, obeying him, and committing yourself firmly to him. This is the key to your life.
>
> Deuteronomy 30:19-20

EPILOGUE

Since Jerry's passing on May 2, 2005, the saying "be careful what you pray for" has certainly proved true in my life. In deep grief, I prayed, "Lord, since you welcomed the love of my life to heaven and you left me here, would you please keep me busy?" He answered my prayer in ways only he could orchestrate. The mind of man could not have manipulated the events that followed.

After learning my first book, *Sins of a Father—Forgiving the Unforgivable*, would go out of print in 2006, I was heartbroken. *Lord, I pled, please don't let this book die. Not because I'm its author, but because of the mounting evidence you are touching so many lives with it. I don't understand.* But God let it die, and it went out of print as scheduled.

At a Christmas day dinner hosted by Doug and Sandy Ross in their home that same year, I sat next to Piotr Waclawik, a publisher from Warsaw, Poland, who had a branch office in Phoenix, Arizona. Doug, president emeritus of Evangelical Christian Publishers Association and a long-time friend of Piotr, urged him to read my book with the idea of republishing it. Piotr graciously requested my book. (How could he not? He hadn't had dessert yet.) While retrieving a copy from my car, I thought, *This is another exercise in futility.* I had tried many times to find another publisher for my book, but no one was interested in reprints. I understood the publishing world and felt sorry for Piotr. *Poor Piotr—publishers are always being put on the spot about publishing some book that the world just can't live without.* Embarrassed, I handed it to Piotr, who glanced at it and politely asked what it was about. When he heard the word *forgive*, he suddenly lit up and excitedly announced, "All of Eastern Europe is begging for anything in print about forgiveness." He said he would read it and asked if I would be willing to go to Poland and speak. I thought, *Yeah, right. Like that's ever going to happen.* But I would have agreed to go to the moon if it would help my book get into print again, so I blithely said, "Of course."

A year later, as a result of that dinner—one which I almost didn't attend—I signed a contract with Piotr Waclawik, CEO of Vocatio Publishers in Warsaw, Poland. How could I know that this God-orchestrated "chance" meeting would result in such far-reaching events?

Following my book's translation into Polish, with a new cover and title, *I Can Forgive If I Want to—Forgiving the Unforgivable,* it was released in Poland. Even before its release, Jagoda Markiewicz, director of Women's Forums in Poland and a staff member of Campus Crusade for Christ, contacted me. She had read the book (in English) I'd given to Piotr, "loved it," and asked if I would consider being the keynote speaker at a number of her annual women's forums the following year. At my stunned silence, she continued. "Please check your schedule, pray about it, and I'll contact you later." It sounded wonderful, but I was hesitant. I would be traveling to Poland alone, be there for a month, and I had never been to Europe. *Lord! I just asked you to not let my book die—I didn't know you'd ask me to go half way across the globe to speak! And why me? There are thousands of authors with far greater accomplishments who are much more qualified than I who would love to make this trip. And I'm sure they wouldn't be as wimpy as I—you know how terrified I am.* God was silent. He knew I would go to Poland and discover my answer there. When Jagoda contacted me, my head swam and my heart pounded, but I said, "Yes."

I arrived in Poland September 29, 2009. At my kick-off speaking event in Warsaw, a personal representative was sent by Elzbieta Radziszewska, head of Poland's State Department, to officially welcome me to her country. Ms. Radziszewska had read my book, and in her welcome, she expressed thanks for its message addressing domestic violence and also offering hope and healing to victims. She then officially endorsed my speaking events in the thirteen cities listed in the promo material. In addition to my speaking engagements that month, I was also a guest on eight radio shows and was interviewed by numerous magazine and newspaper reporters who had each read my entire book before interviewing me. (That in itself amazed me! I'd been interviewed by one television talk show host in the States who hadn't even read my book!) As I wondered what in my book so interested the media, I began to suspect the reason for my trip.

At that time, Poland was just becoming aware of the prevalence of domestic violence and its impact on their society. I didn't know this prior to my trip, but once I realized this fact, every city in which I spoke, I strongly encouraged them to provide women's shelters and safe houses. "Victims need a place of refuge where they and their children can go and feel safe. As you know," I told them, "Polish women are being killed because they can't escape their abusers."

I had already heard numerous stories from Polish women who, through tears, related their terrifying experiences. It took one woman seven years to obtain a divorce from her abusive husband. The few shelters available (provided by the Catholic Church) were located only in the large cities. I shared the terror my family and I had felt at being held captive in our abusive environment. There were no shelters to offer us safety. I suggested they push for local government agencies to provide aid and legal assistance for abuse victims. I told them how far the United States had come since I was a child and how shelters and assistance programs are available almost everywhere.

I was moved by the many women who brought their books for me to sign, after showing me the numerous pages where much of the text was highlighted. Many commented they had read the book several times, with one woman proudly proclaiming she was on her fifth reading. Many wept and thanked me for writing the book and showing them how to forgive.

The Polish people opened their homes and hearts to me. Everywhere I spoke, in public and private, they were eager to hear my words of hope and hungry for God's presence. Many openly wept as I spoke via the translators. Just as I began to suspect why I was the messenger God chose for this trip, Jagoda and I arrived in the city of Kolo (pronounced Kovo). Dorotha Laskowski, women's director of that large event (which was covered in the local evening television news where she was interviewed with scenes of Jagoda and me speaking in the background) greeted us with the customary Polish greeting—a kiss to each cheek. Dorotha was the one God chose to answer my question of "Why me?"

Still clutching both my arms tightly, she leaned in closer. Fighting for composure, her intense, tear-filled eyes riveted on mine, she announced, "I have been praying for six years that God would send someone to Poland with the message of forgiveness. Thank you for being willing to travel so far to answer that prayer."

There's your answer, the Lord whispered.

As I toured Auschwitz and relived the horrors of the holocaust, my heart broke for that great country—a brave nation that had been beaten and brutalized by its neighbors throughout its entire existence. I recall thinking, *Poland has rebuilt its beautiful cities, but the healing of its soul is a longer process*. I felt humbled to be there at a time when God was stirring that nation's heart toward healing that comes only through forgiveness. By the time I returned home to America, I had fallen in love with the Polish people, and part of my heart remained in Poland.

Since that trip, God keeps leading me into Polish communities. I was keynote speaker at a Polish family conference held in Las Vegas, Nevada, where over seven thousand Poles reside, as well as at two Polish conferences in New Jersey and New York.

As Christians, we are familiar with God's promise in Isaiah 65:25, which tells us that even before we call, God will answer.

Before my trip to Poland I wished a number of times that I could learn at least a little Polish. Just some simple phrases and words, such as "Where is the bathroom?" "Where is the American Embassy?" and "Help!" Since I didn't want to learn the entire language, I had no desire—or time for that matter—I never even considered praying about it. But that's okay. As usual, God had me covered.

My friend Staci Charles, Founder & Chief Marketing Strategist of Brain Lab, called saying she understood I was going to Poland and invited me to join her and two Polish friends for lunch. There she introduced me to Ania Kubicki, ANGLES Public Relations, and her mother, Halina Pennar. They were originally from Krakow and had been citizens in the United States since Ania was a child.

Midway through lunch, Halina smiled and offered, "I am a certified Polish instructor, and I would love to tutor you in Polish before your trip." I gladly accepted. That was late in 2008 before my trip to Poland in the fall of 2009. *You did it again, Lord,* I thought, mentally shaking my head. He had provided for this need even without my asking. So like him! As an added bonus, Halina and I became the best of friends. She and her family have "adopted" me and include me in many of their family activities. (My two children, David with his wife, Kim, and my daughter, Tamara, as well as my granddaughter, Bailey, all live in California, and I have no family here.) I was blessed further when Halina later moved to less than a mile from me.

Another need answered, but one I prayed for: Before leaving for Poland I had prayed, "Lord, I need a friend in my neighborhood—someone to just have coffee with once in a while when I need a break from my busy schedule." My neighbors were nice, but they all worked and were busy with their families.

After I returned from Poland, my doorbell rang, and a young couple two doors down who had just recently moved in told me of an early morning water leak in my yard I was unaware of. After inviting them in, Sylvia noted my Polish books on the coffee table and asked excitedly, "Are you Polish? I was born in Krakow. My family and I moved here when I was very young and we all became citizens."

I explained about my trip. She and her husband, Robert, welcomed me immediately into their hearts and lives, and we've become steadfast friends. I admitted one day to Sylvia, barely in her thirties, that she was my answer to prayer. She responded, "You're my answer to prayer too—I've wanted someone like you in my life." This young couple had their first baby last year, so now I am their beautiful little Sophia's *babcia* (grandmother).

Since Jerry's passing, God has also busied me with my writing. Approximately twenty-five of my nonfiction stories have been published in compilation books. My book *Good Mews—Inspurrrational Stories for Cat Lovers* was released by Thomas Nelson Publishers. The devotionals in this book are all true stories involving the pet cats Jerry and I had throughout our forty-seven years of marriage. (Jerry absolutely loved this book!) These are not just fluff-and-fill stories about cats who do "cat things" with a Scripture tossed in to match the story. These are poignant accounts of lessons I learned from God while trying to teach our cats something. During each incident, it was as though God thumped me on the head and said, "Uh huh, and who does that remind you of?"

I've also published one e-book, *Friendship—When It's Easy and When It's Not.*

Though Piotr closed his Phoenix office and returned to Poland before my book was again released here in the United States, he is responsible for it being published in Polish, Dutch, Nepali, Finnish, and its recent release in Mumbai, India.

I am blessed and grateful that Tate Publishers is the United States' publisher of this updated version, again, something orchestrated by God.

The latest door God is opening, as only he can do, is a possible movie of this book. Again, Poland is involved.

Through Jagoda, a Brazilian/Polish filmmaker read this book and was convinced it should be made into a feature film. It is because of his enthusiastic encouragement that steps are underway by a U.S. director and screenwriter to make this project a reality.

I will never understand how God works, nor am I supposed to, for his ways truly are mysterious. But in looking back at the death, rebirth, and evolvement of my book, I am reminded of the statement made by Jesus in John 12:24, "Unless a kernel of wheat is planted in the soil and dies, it remains alone. But its death will produce many new kernels—a plentiful harvest of new lives."

As painful as it was for me at the time, had my *Sins of a Father* book not died and gone out of print, *I Can Forgive if I Want To* would never have been born, nor would it be in other languages; this timely European trip would not have happened, and thousands of people in Poland would have missed the blessing of its message of forgiveness. Nor would this current book have found its timely way to Tate Publishers or into your hands.

Through faithful prayers and focused positive attitudes, we too, as the legendary phoenix, can rise above the ashes of our past and soar into unbelievable realms as we become all that God created us to be.

DOMESTIC VIOLENCE

Each year our nation recognizes October as Domestic Violence Awareness Month. Five brief articles on domestic violence, written by Kitty Chappell under contract to online publisher Genius Avenue, LLC, are reprinted below with permission. While not extensive, each article provides valuable information and data that could save someone's life—maybe yours.

DOMESTIC VIOLENCE: POWER AND CONTROL

The U. S. Office on Violence against Women defines domestic violence as a "pattern of abusive behavior in any relationship that is used by one partner to gain or maintain power and control over another intimate partner." It can take many forms, including physical, sexual, emotional, economic, and psychological abuse.

Who are the victims? Anyone. The Domestic Violence Resource Center reports that each year in the United States between 600,000 and 6 million women are victims of abuse—and between 100,000 and 6 million men, depending on the type of survey used. Because our culture demands that men present a strong façade, this leads to minimizing female-perpetrated abuse; thus, those figures are harder to quantify. These figures, though, speak volumes:

- On average, every day in America more than three women and one man are murdered by their intimate partners (IP). In 2000, 1,247 women were killed by an IP. The same year, 440 men lost their lives to an IP.

- Costs of intimate partner violence in the United States exceed $5.8 billion annually. $4.1 billion are for direct medical and health care services. Productivity losses account for nearly $1.8 billion.

- Four children die every day in America from child abuse and neglect.

- This nation spends approximately $258 million annually on foster care, incarceration, and other costs due to child abuse and neglect.

- Forty-five percent of abused children become adult alcoholics, continuing the cycle of abuse.

These statistics reveal an urgent need for intervention for the abused and abuser. What can you and I do? First and foremost, we can educate ourselves. Then we must be willing and courageous enough to help.

Would you recognize abusive tendencies in your partner? We'll cover that topic next.

(Originally published online by Genius Avenue LLC. Reprinted with permission.)

DOMESTIC VIOLENCE: USE YOUR HEAD, NOT YOUR HEART

As the oldest child in my abused family, I often tried to protect my mother from our father's jealous rages and beatings. At sixteen, I fell in love with and became engaged to a handsome high school dropout—who I hoped was my ticket to freedom! Initially, I was flattered by his extreme possessiveness...until my male schoolmates started avoiding me, some sporting black eyes and bandaged noses. Though my fiancé never hit me, I saw too many of my father's traits in him, so I ditched him. I didn't want to repeat my mother's mistake.

But how many young women *don't* see the signs?

Noticing and acknowledging warning signs and symptoms of domestic violence is the first step to preventing it—and ending it. No one should live in fear of the person they love.

Here are a few of the most common warning signs. If you recognize any of these in your intimate relationships, take action.

Does your partner (male or female) ever...

- act excessively jealous and possessive?

- put you down and make you feel worthless?

- intimidate and threaten to hurt you or someone you love?

- threaten to hurt himself/herself if you don't comply with their wishes?

- try to isolate you from your friends or family?

- abuse you, then act loving, saying it won't happen again, but it does?

- pressure or force you into unwanted sex?

- control your access to money?

- stalk you, including calling you constantly or following you?

If you suspect you are in an abusive relationship, be assured there is help available in your community. Call 800-621-HOPE (4673).

(Originally published online by Genius Avenue LLC. Reprinted with permission.)

GETTING AWAY FROM DOMESTIC ABUSE: A PEEK BEHIND THE DOOR

You are told by your abuser that you can't survive without him because you're stupid and unemployable—and he blames *you* for his abuse. Despite the small voice crying inside you, saying, "It's not true," his abuse validates his destructive words, and you believe him.

How do I know? Because, for years, I heard such comments from my father as he abused me, my siblings, and my mother. We were freed from him only after his imprisonment for almost murdering my mother.

Why didn't we leave? There was no place to go. At that time, there were no domestic violence organizations to aid victims. Thankfully, that's no longer true.

Where to Find Help

Today, there are local abuse organizations that provide safe shelter, counseling, occupational training, help you find employment, direct you to either free or affordable legal counsel, and even accompany you as you face your adversary during your divorce proceeding. *But leaving your abusive environment must begin with you.* Don't make the mistake of doing nothing or merely trying harder to please your abuser in hopes he will improve. Statistically, abusers never change until separated from their victims, if then. Check your local telephone directory for domestic violence services.

Safety Alert

If you are in danger, call 911, your local hotline, or the U.S. National Domestic Violence Hotline (NDVH) at 1-800-799-7233 and TTY 1-800-787-3224. If in no immediate danger, contact NDVH by computer at thehotline.org for helpful information. Be sure to use a safe computer at a different location, as anything you research will leave a computer trail, which you won't want your abuser to follow.

There are trained professionals who genuinely care about you and are waiting for your call.

(Originally published online by Genius Avenue LLC. Reprinted with permission.)

MOVING FORWARD FOLLOWING DOMESTIC ABUSE: DON'T STAY STUCK

I thought I'd be happy following my father's imprisonment, but I wasn't. We had relocated to begin our new life and heal from our hurts, but it wasn't working. We had dragged our past with us.

I was the first to tire of rehashing past injustices. Observing how hate kept us chained to my father, and hoping forgiveness might free us, I discussed it with Mom. She said she'd never forgive Dad. He didn't deserve it. I countered, "Forgiveness is for *our* healing, not *his*—don't *we* deserve freedom?"

We the children ultimately forgave Dad and moved on. Mom refused, believing her unforgiveness would cause Dad to suffer. But it didn't. Sadly, Mom never moved forward and stayed stuck in her bitterness until her death.

You can—and should—learn from your past, but don't relive it. Prepare for moving ahead with these four tips:

Mental: Stimulate your mind. Start a new hobby, join a book club, or do puzzles. This can be interesting and build confidence. You'll discover you're *not* dumb, as you were previously told.

Physical: Exercise and walk whenever possible. Get adequate rest. Cut down on alcohol, nicotine, and caffeine. Don't skip meals. Try eating nutritious foods. Many actually do taste good!

Social: Make time for wholesome fun. Select friends who encourage and bring out the best in you. Avoid negative individuals who drain and depress you. Linger around those who laugh easily and make *you* laugh.

Spiritual: Find a church or synagogue to inspire you. Worship provides a beneficial healing dimension, especially for those overcoming abusive backgrounds. You could be surprised—you might not fall asleep during the service.

Remember, you are *irreplaceable*! There will never be another you...so be the best and happiest *you* possible!

(Originally published online by Genius Avenue LLC. Reprinted with permission.)

RESPONDING TO DOMESTIC ABUSE: BASIC AND PRACTICAL SUPPORT

Helping your friends victimized by domestic abuse starts with the basics. Encourage them to talk to people who can provide help and guidance. Offer to go with them to talk with other family and friends. Find a local domestic violence agency that provides counseling or support groups. If they need to go to the police, to court, or to see an attorney, offer to go with them as moral support.

More practical responses include

- Educate yourself through material available at the National Domestic Violence Hotline (NDVH). Google their acronym and click on "Helping a Friend."

- Be supportive and nonjudgmental. Listen. They need someone to believe them.

- Let them know the abuse is not their fault; they didn't cause it.

- Focus on concerns for your friend instead of criticizing the abuser. Your friend may not be receptive to your help if she feels she has to defend why she is in the relationship. Love dies hard and many victims love their abuser.

- Don't try to rescue them. Leaving the relationship must be their decision. If it isn't, they'll likely return to the abuser and things will worsen. Yet be bold in expressing your concern for their safety.

- Prepare yourself for the time they do ask for help by reading NDVH safety planning tips. You can then discuss them with your friend.

- Be supportive when the abused feels alone or mourns the loss of the relationship. This is a normal part of the healing process.

Finally, you are needed as a *volunteer*! I know older couples who babysit at a local shelter while mothers attend counseling sessions. Do you think those children will ever forget those loving grandparent figures? Why not call your local shelter and offer to help any way you can. What better legacy can you leave than having made a difference in someone's life?

(Originally published online by Genius Avenue LLC. Reprinted with permission.)

PHOTOS

Clyde Caudle and his horse, Star – overseeing large farm in Red River Bottoms as foreman - 1940.

Kitty, Chuck, & Esther in Fulton, AR - 1941.

Esther Watson-Caudle and her younger brother, Paul Watson. This was Kitty's Uncle who invited her to church the night her life changed forever – 1942

Kitty, Chris, and Chuck Caudle – 1943

Chris, Chuck, & Kitty Caudle – 1946

Chris and Chuck Caudle with Cocoa, the goat, at McAllister farm – 1947

Grandpa Willie McAllister's farmhouse near
Hatfield, AR - the Caudle children's heaven away
from hell.

Granny Watson-McAllister and Grandpa "Willie"
with smiles as big as their hearts.

Esther Watson-Caudle, who subsidized the family income as seamstress, made both of these outfits. Her two-piece dress was made of rayon acetate and lined with satin – 1950

Caudle family at 1618 Oak Street in Texarkana, TX - 1951

Renovated Oak Street home in Texarkana, TX in 2003. The Caudles lived there from 1944 until early 1952 when they moved to 2116 Blvd where Clyde almost murdered Esther. While attending her Texarkana, Texas High School 50th Class Reunion in 2003, Kitty visited the old Boulevard home site only to discover it had been replaced with an E-Z Mart.

Chris, Esther, Kitty, and Chuck Caudle – 1953

1953 – Esther-Watson-Caudle at age 34, posing in Kitty's high school prom dress. Having finished only the 4th grade, Esther never had a prom dress of her own.

Kitty & Chris with family pet ducks, Donald and Daisy – 1954 (168 KB)

Texarkana Post Office/
Court House where in 1955
Clyde was tried for Esther's
attempted murder.

Chris & Chuck in 1958 enjoying
freedom in Santa Barbara, CA after
Clyde's imprisonment.

David, Kitty, Jerry, and Tamara Chappell enjoying Christmas in the 1970's.

Esther Watson-Caudle-Hayes and second husband, Ira, in the 1980's.

Clyde Caudle and second wife, Mary Wilma
Cawrse-Caudle - 1987.

Kitty Caudle-Chappell, Clyde Caudle, and Chris
Caudle-Brown, taken at Clyde's and Mary's home
in Mentone, California - 1988.

Mary Wilma Caudle with Kitty and Chris during their
1988 visit.

Kitty, Clyde Caudle, and Kitty's daughter, Tamara
Chappell, taken in the Chappell home five months
before Clyde murdered his second wife, Mary Wilma,
and then committed suicide - 1989.

Couple found dead in murder-suicide

By 'A BORGATTA
Sta. /riter

November 2, 1989

MENTONE — An elderly Mentone man apparently shot and killed his wife and then committed suicide earlier this week, according to a San Bernardino Sheriff's Department spokesman.

The couple — Clyde Caudle, 75, and his wife Mary, 55 — were discovered by sheriff's deputies about 10:23 p.m. Wednesday, said Jim Bryant, the department's public information officer.

Caudle and his wife had been hospitalized in August after an earlier incident. Caudle ran his car off a highway, and the Sheriff's Department investigated the accident as an attempted murder-suicide.

On Wednesday, deputies went to the Caudles' home, located at 1361 Beryl St., to serve an arrest warrant for the 75-year-old man in connection to the August incident, Bryant said.

When the deputies received no response at the door, they forced entry into the house and found the cou▮ ▮ead of gunshot wounds, the spok▮ ▮an said.

Sheriff's homicide investigators were called to the scene, and through an initial investigation they determined that Caudle shot his wife and then himself, according to Sgt. Larry Brown of the sheriff's homicide detail. It appeared the couple had been dead for several days, Brown.

Caudle's first murder and suicide attempt was made on Aug. 13 when he and his wife were returning home from the Big Bear area, a sheriff's department spokesman said at the time.

While traveling westbound on State Route 18, Caudle reportedly initiated a U-turn and drove the vehicle off the roadway.

Caudle's wife was thrown from the vehicle about 200 feet from the side of the highway and was transported to Big Bear Valley Hospital for treatment, the spokesman said.

Caudle received treatment at Loma Linda University Hospital, he said.

Caudle had reportedly been despondent over his affliction with Parkinson's Disease, a condition which affects the nervous system.

The couple were apparently living together at the time of the shooting.

Murder-suicide article.

SHERIFF'S DEPARTMENT

County of San Bernardino
California

CA 03600

CASE NO.
89095155-04

REPORT AREA

PAGE FOUR

E SECTION	CRIME	CLASSIFICATION	
PC 187	MURDER/SUICIDE	SHOOTING	
IM'S NAME — LAST NAME	FIRST NAME	MIDDLE NAME	(FIRM NAME IF BUSINESS)
CAUDLE,	MARY		
RESS	RESIDENCE	BUSINESS	PHONE ( )

ADDITIONAL INFORMATION OFFICER:

After obtaining neighborhood contacts, I went to the crime scene and assisted Det. Terrell and Ingersoll in doing the crime scene investigation.

ADDITIONAL INTERVIEWS:

On Thursday, 11-2-89 at approximately 1015 hours, Det. Snyder gave me information that ✕ from Mentone had called with some additional information reference the Caudle's. At 1050 hours, 11-2-89, I made contact with Mr. ✕ at his residence in Mentone where I obtained the following interview.

✕ Mill Creek Rd., Mentone (home) ✕ (work) ✕

Mr. ✕ told me he used to be neighbors with the Caudles and when they would go on trips he would watch their house. ✕ said after the wreck in Big Bear last summer, just before Mr. Caudle was due to be released from the hospital, Mrs. Caudle brought over three suitcases full of clothes to the ✕ residence and told them that she wanted to keep the suitcases there I case she needed to make a quick getaway. Mr. ✕ told me that he still in fact has all three suitcases. Mr. ✕ told me he would make contact with Caudle's son and release the suitcases to him.

described Mrs. Caudle's attitude toward her husband as being very afraid of him and he also described them as being a very strange couple. I asked him to elaborate on this and he told me the Caudle's were very quiet and did not socialize with anybody. Mr. ✕ told me he has known the Caudle's for approximately 20 years and other than having periodic short conversations with them, he does not know very much about them. ✕ said he has not talked to Mrs. Caudle, but knows that his wife has and he did not know about any guns. He said it has been several weeks since he has heard from either one of the Caudle's.

NG OFFICERS	DATE	REVIEWED BY	TYPED BY	ROUTED BY	DATE
). Finneran F0359	110389		pat		

THER ACTION:	COPIES TO:			REMARKS
] YES] NO	Detective	SD/PD	Other	
	CII	Other		
184-401 Rev 1 '83	Dist. Atty.	Patrol		

Sheriff's Department Report, Page four

Jerry & Kitty Chappell – 2000

Jerry and Kitty's two children, daughter, Tamara, and son, David, with Kitty at Jerry's funeral service May 2, 2005.

Chris Caudle-Kotecki-Brown & husband, Everett

Chuck Caudle and wife, Nancy

David Chappell and wife, Kim

Bailey Rachelle Chappell – Only grandchild of Jerry and Kitty - and their son David's only child with his first wife, Tricia. Bailey never had a squirrel and dumpling supper prepared by Grandma Kitty.